Modern Witchcraft

Modern Witchcraft

THE FASCINATING STORY OF THE REBIRTH OF PAGANISM AND MAGIC

FRANK SMYTH

CASTLE BOOKS

To Michael Bakewell and Diana Tyler without whom . . .

This book was originally published in England by Macdonald Unit 75. It is here reprinted by arrangement.

Contents

I

Witchcraft Today

'A WITCH of full powers is urgently sought to lift a 73-year-old curse and help restore the family fortunes of an afflicted nobleman. Employment genuinely offered.'

This was the text of an advertisment which appeared in the London *Times* of March 11, 1967. The advertiser, as the London *Sunday Express* revealed some days later, was the 74-year-old Duke of Leinster, head of one of Britain's oldest families. Over 170 people offered to help; one of them was 68-year-old Magda Buchel, a cousin of the Duke of Norfolk, the hereditary Earl Marshal of England – the Duke's duties in recent years have included the 'stage management' of the last Coronation, the funeral of Sir Winston Churchill, and the installation of Prince Charles as Prince of Wales.

Two weeks before the Duke of Leinster's advertisement was published, a Turkish-Cypriot woman in her early thirties had appeared at the Old Bailey, London, accused of demanding £90 with menaces and with stealing £70 from one of her fellow countrywomen. The accused was alleged to have gained the money by telling her friend that unless an expensive spell were cast, a 'Satanic curse' which had been laid upon her children would take effect, and the children would inevitably die. The accused then ladled seven spoonfuls of water into a basin, took an egg, wrapped it in white cloth, and broke it under the leg of her victim with the same spoon, crying 'Diabolo, Diabolo' as she did so. If the egg contained blood and worms, she explained, nothing could be done. As it was, the egg contained what the accused said was human hair, and the 'curse' was lifted.

Two curses, two entirely different backgrounds. But both believed in England, in the latter half of the 20th century. In fact the power to curse, to blight another's life, love, or means of living by magic has been a constant fear throughout the centuries. 'We are all afraid of being nailed by spells and dire curses,' said Pliny the Elder, writing in the first century AD, and his observation seems to have been true ever since.

The European mind tends nowadays to equate the word 'witchcraft' with 'savagery', with the mumbo jumbo of African witchdoctors, or the bone-pointing of Australian aborigines, or the heart-devouring rituals of the ancient Incas. And yet witchcraft, sorcery, magic, superstition, is as deep-rooted a tradition of Germany or Scotland, for instance, as it is of central Africa or the jungles of Brazil. Every time you 'touch wood' for luck, you are unconsciously invoking the old, primeval forest gods; every time you avoid walking under a ladder you are respecting the sacred triangle, the mystic number three of Egyptian numerology. Spill salt, we are told, and bad luck falls upon us; for in the old days salt, the preserver of meat throughout long winter months, was an extremely valuable commodity. Roman soldiers often received half of their pay in salt, hence the modern word 'salary'. Of course, to counteract the effect of spilling salt, one should take a pinch of the salt and fling it over the left shoulder without looking around. The Greeks, among other peoples, believed that two spirits walked behind every individual. One, on the right, was a good influence, the other was bad. The spilling of salt, the symbol of life, enabled the evil spirit to gain the upper hand, but salt thrown in his face deterred him.

These are superstitions common in most European countries, as well as in most other parts of the world. The motives, and the fears, behind each one of them had their origins in the basic thinking of mankind, not merely in the culture of a particular ethnic group.

The power of the enchanter's eye is feared today almost as much as it ever was in most parts of the world, east and west. To the Italians, the *mal occhio* is still a potential danger which is warded off by extending the little and index fingers of the left hand and pointing them at the possessor of the 'evil eye', at the same time spitting on the ground. In France, the *mauvais oeuil* is defied by making the sign of the cross; the same sign protects Germans from the *böse Blick*. In the British Isles, particularly in Ireland, Scotland, and the West Country, the fear of cattle or pigs being 'overlooked' by the evil eye lingers on in the minds of many farmers, in the same way that the lucky horseshoe, an old amulet against 'fascination', remains fixed over the doors of even the most up-to-date farm. In modern Israel, Hebrew-speaking Jews – though often apostate – remain wary of the *ayn – hara*, perhaps remembering the Biblical injunction 'eat thou not the bread of him that hath an evil eye'.

Nor is superstition and the fear of witchcraft easy to eradicate. An official of the Russian Embassy in London told me recently that superstition, along with organised religion, had been abolished from the USSR in 1917. He would have no truck with any of it, he said. Three hours and several drinks later, he told me that he was married to a Georgian girl. 'When I married her, I and her parents followed the old Georgian custom of piling thick pancakes in the centre of the table,' he told me. 'The pancakes are sliced like a cake into wedges, one wedge for each member of the wedding party. But the bridegroom, in this case myself, had to eat the portion – about ten pancakes thick – at one sitting, and then drink a large tumbler of vodka off in one go. In the old days, the gods helped a man to accomplish this task of trenchermanship; if he was worthy of his bride, then he would achieve what was required of him. If not, he was rejected by both father-in-law and bride alike.'

I suggested to the Russian that this custom, with its 'plea to the gods' aspect, was unworthy of his Marxist principles; he quickly denied that any 'supernatural' element was present. The practice, he said, was merely a 'quaint old custom' carried on by his father and grandfather before him. It was in vain to point out that the practice of touching wood carried on by Christians carried similar undertones and that both pancake eating and wood touching involved the forgotten invocation of old gods.

Even Communist China, the strictest of all the world's left wing cultures, is reported to have difficulty in suppressing the beliefs in magic which had their origin in the mystical Shang Dynasty of 3,000 years ago. Although ancestor worship is now against the law, millions of Chinese find it hard to forget their hitherto honoured forebears, while acupuncture – the ancient system of curing all disease by inserting golden needles lightly under certain points of the skin – still thrives in many parts of the country, along with the elaborate rituals which have surrounded its practice for generations.

A celebrated Belgian journalist who has a greater knowledge than most Westerners of conditions in modern China tells the story of how he approached a high ranking official in charge of one of the major museums in Peking and asked for information on dragons.

Dragons, and references to dragons, he was told politely but firmly, had been expunged from the lore of China. They were part of the Imperialist past, and should not be mentioned. The journalist expressed disappointment at this information. He had been considering writing a book entitled 'The Feathered Dragon'.

'But that is sheer nonsense,' said the high ranking official, 'everyone knows that dragons don't have feathers!'

If the Communist bloc have difficulty in severing the superstitious past from the highly technological present, the Western world, which is still nominally religious, manifests even deeper involvement with the beliefs of centuries ago. In West Berlin, books of spells and magical rituals vie with pornography for pride of place in the red light areas of the city.

In France, a fixation with love charms reflects that country's reputation for gentle, idyllic romance as well as sexual passion. In America, where a couple of generations ago people of all nations sought a new, bright future, the descendants of those pioneers are now seeking out the magical traditions of their past. The film *Rosemary's Baby* became one of the biggest box office draws of all time almost overnight and when, months after its release, the wife of its director became the tragic, eponymous centre of the 'Sharon Tate Murders', the eyes of the world turned disbelievingly to California, scene of the crime. For according to newspaper reports Miss Tate's killers had been members of a drug-crazed, semi-mystical group who called themselves the 'Cult of Satan', or 'Satan's Slaves'.

But perhaps oddest of all the new, occult trends which are sweeping the Western world today is that which is receiving more and more attention in Great Britain – traditional land, to foreigners, of the stiff-upper-lip and no-nonsense, unemotional conservatism. Witchcraft, relegated to the realm of children's fantasy for years, has once more come into its own as a thriving cult: so much so, in fact, that more than one Member of Parliament has called for the re-introduction of legislation against the movement. Whether such legislation will ever appear on the statute books remains to be seen; what is certain is that witchcraft as a way of life appeals to more and more British men and women every day.

2

Witchcraft in Britain

DESPITE the fact that superstition has always been with us, the last few years of the 1960s saw a flowering of interest in occult matters which would have been inexplicable to an earlier generation: the forties and early fifties were sternly practical times, overshadowed by war and the dogged recovery from its effects. Astrologers, had, of course, played a minor part in the war effort of both sides. In 1947 a small mention was made of the death, through drugs, drink, and general excess, of Aleister Crowley, the 'Great Beast'. In 1951, the Witchcraft Act of 1735 was repealed and replaced by the Fraudulent Mediums Act and, with the relaxation of restrictions on newsprint, the sensational Sundays were able, in the early fifties, to regale their readers with cautionary tales about the ill-defined 'dangers' of dabbling with the supernatural.

But that, in the immediate post-war era, was as far as the supernatural went. To a society newly emerged from the valley of the shadow of death, the Black Market was far more interesting than the Black Mass.

Now, twenty years later, it seems scarcely possible to

pick up a newspaper or turn on a television set without some reference being made to ghosts, demons, magicians, or witches. The occult, which lay dormant for so many years, is once again up and thriving all around us. The interest in astrology, starting with newspaper horoscopes and ending with the increased sales of large and expensive books on the subject, is perhaps the most spectacular indication of the widespread hold which the supernatural has taken on the imagination of modern society. The horoscopes published in most newspapers and magazines are among the most popular features, and many people turn directly to them; nor are they always treated as mere 'fun' for many believers use them as a general guide to their affairs.

In 1969 it was estimated that there were about 10,000 full-time and 175,000 part-time astrologers in the United States, while in Britain the number of professionals was increasing. Patric Walker, who writes as 'Novalis' in *Nova* and was responsible for the *Daily Mirror* colour supplement horoscope, reported that businessmen, actors, sportsmen, and professional people from all walks of life were increasingly consulting the stars as a guide to their fortunes. And it is not insignificant that the top box-office draw in recent years has been the hit musical *Hair* during which thousands of theatre-goers are strangely comforted and simultaneously thrilled by the words of 'Aquarius':

> When the moon is in the seventh house,
> And Jupiter allies with Mars
> Then peace will guide the planets,
> And love will steer the stars.

The Press have always been conscious of the selling power of the unknown, and with the resurgence of interest, newspapers of all kinds started digging into their files with the result that today the supernatural stands firmly alongside Royalty, animals, and sex as one of the great Fleet Street selling subjects. Ghosts, particularly that boisterous influence the poltergeist, have never ceased to be good for a few paragraphs on page three, along with features about 'Life After Death – Does the Soul Survive?' simply because everyone has at least a passing interest in his prospects in the 'great beyond'. Now that science, in the form of such organisations as the Institute of Psychophysical Research at Oxford, Duke University in the USA, and various investigating bodies in the Soviet Union, is beginning to look closely into psychic phenomena, apparitions of all kinds have taken on a new respectability.

But of all occult subjects the most fascinating one to the 20th-century mind is that of witchcraft. Witches, long ago relegated by most people to the level of the fairy tale, have suddenly cropped up again. Certainly it comes as quite a surprise to learn that, amidst the white heat of technology and in a countryside covered with the acne of housing estates, nude witches continue to carry out the ancient craft. And not in secret, either. Witches appear on the 'David Frost Show', they chat with Joan Bakewell on 'Late Night Line-up', and have their say in the glossy pages of women's magazines. Nor are they in any way ashamed of their beliefs and practices. Witchcraft, they claim, is the true religion of Europe, usurped by Christianity but never completely killed by it. It is the worship of the creative forces of the universe, the recognition of the two halves which make up the whole, the bringing together of male and female, Yin and Yang, right and wrong, black and white. It is also the means whereby mankind is able to tap the ancient forces of creation, the magical powers of centuries ago, translate them into physical terms, and use them for good or ill. In other words, they believe that, like their counterparts in Grimm's fairy tales, they can cast spells.

The word 'witch' comes from the Middle English word 'wicca' meaning 'wise'; it is interesting to know that the word 'wicked' and the dialect word 'wick' meaning 'alive' or 'life' come from the same source. Because of the root-word, modern witches refer to their religion as the 'Cult of Wicca'. Although some of them have differences of opinion about minor matters of ritual their basic end is the same: the worship of the mother goddess and horned god of the ancients, who symbolise to the witches the basic universal creative forces, and the practice of magic which, they unanimously state, they use only for good. Witches believe that any act of magic rebounds thrice-fold on the operator, so that their attachment to 'white' witchcraft is prudent as well as philanthropic. The difference between a witch and a magician is always emphasised by the former. Most modern ritual magicians are unconcerned with worship, and occupy their time in bending elementals and other supernatural powers to do their will and thus endow them with material 'power'. Although witches also practise magic, their emphasis is on the religious aspect of their beliefs; above all else modern witches strive for respectability in the eyes of society at large.

Before considering in detail the beliefs and practices of 'wicca' and attempting to relate them to their counterparts in other countries and in other times, it may be interesting to look at them as a social group because, perhaps not surprisingly, they do tend to be alike in many respects outside their mutual religion. Estimates of their numbers have varied between 6,000 and 'a mere handful'; in fact, judging by letters and interviews and by research carried out prior to the launching of the part-work magazine *Man, Myth and Magic*, it is fairly safe to say that about 600 people attend 'coven' meetings in Scotland, Wales, and England today, and a small growing number of Americans are also members of the 'wicca' cult. In Ireland, perhaps because of the strong hold which both the Catholic and Protestant Churches still have there, few witch groups exist. It is this relatively small number which causes much of the similarity between witchcraft believers: in a word, they know each other. And they all tend to fall into the same social class. They number among their naked ranks schoolteachers, book-keepers, policemen, at least one stage conjurer, salesmen and, despite the frequent antagonism of the Press, one or two local journalists. All in all they fall into what advertising men refer to as the 'CD' stream of society; if spiritualism is the prerogative of the decaying nobility of South Kensington and the working classes of

Kentish Town, then British witches can usually be relied on to be lower middle class.

Because of their inherent similarity it is tempting to generalise about the witchcraft fraternity in Britain today, and, unlike most generalisations, those relating to modern witches rarely seem to fall wide of the mark. For two years, between 1968 and 1970 I spoke to two or three dozen of them, in different parts of the country, and both myself and my various assistants formed identical and very firm impressions. For instance, one small point – but a most noticeable one – is that most of them tend to drink sherry – Cyprus or Australian sherry rather than Portuguese. There is no obvious reason for this; it is true that sherry is often used by covens in what they term a 'cakes and wine' ceremony, but on the other hand one would hardly expect to be offered altar wine by a Catholic priest, for example, when visiting his home socially. One High Priestess interviewed during a three-hour-long evening session refused Scotch, brought by the interviewer, and instead demolished two bottles of sweet South African all by herself.

Again, the politics of witchcraft tend to be much of a muchness – fairly right wing – although perhaps conservatism is inevitable in people who claim to be carrying on a three-thousand-year-old tradition. In all my talks I met only two Socialist witches, and of the rest about ninety per cent were pro-Powell in differing degrees. One man in Highgate said: 'I wouldn't admit coloured people to our meetings, simply because they have different traditions of witchcraft, and they wouldn't harmonise with us. I'm not biased of course, but that is the way it is. A foreigner could upset all our members and break the whole thing up.' A lady sorcerer in London was more explicit: 'I would never teach magic to a black or anyone else of an inferior race. They haven't the intelligence, and in the wrong hands magic can do untold harm.'

The habitat of the average witch is as mundane and cosy as his drinking habits. Semis, red-brick Edwardian terraced houses, and flats in the suburbs are, predictably enough, the usual scene of coven meetings, though one or two believers are fortunate to own atmospheric country cottages with heavy beams and outdoor sanitation. The decor of the typical witch's home tends to reflect the 'Craft's' love of elaborate ornament; pictures of Horned God figures, African ju-ju carvings, Egyptian scarabs, crystal balls, Maori spears, and ritual swords and daggers all jostle for pride of place among Tretchikoff prints and formations of plaster ducks. More than one witch shows a glimmer of humour by having little witch dolls or demons propped up on the mantelpiece, and a Sheffield husband and wife team display a traditional witch's broom in their front porch.

Witches themselves are, politics apart, a fairly friendly crowd. Despite the predominantly youthful interest in the occult generally, the followers of 'wicca' are for the most part in their late thirties and forties, Grammar school and Technical college educated, with a wide though frequently shallow and ill-digested knowledge of the magical traditions. They are not normally given to open proselytism and, in view of the current interest in their practices, they do not need to be – would-be converts seek them out. Nor are they, on the surface at least, fanatical in their beliefs, despite the fact that anonymous, frequently vitriolic letters threatening the author with all manner of supernatural afflictions quickly follow any criticism of modern witchcraft in the Press.

The Press, of course, more than any other medium, has formed the general public's impression of what motivates the British witch today, and that impression generally has sex as its pre-eminent feature. In spring 1969 the *News of the World*, putting on its guardian-of-the-public-morals hat, published a series of articles which lumped together witchcraft, ritual magic, the Black Mass, and the desecration of churchyards by vandals. During the course of this series the paper uncovered the facts that a schoolteacher-priest had planned to hold Black Masses using virgins as an altar, that a couple in the Isle of Man exposed their young daughter to the danger of moral corruption by allowing her to attend naked coven meetings, and that a West London housewife had been the prime mover at similar coven meetings for years without the knowledge of her husband. If the first two allegations were true, of course, the *News of the World* performed a public service by exposing them. But by and large the articles tended to overdo the sexual aspect of 'wicca'.

It is undeniably true that sex played a major part, if the evidence at the witch trials of the Middle Ages is to be believed, in the witchcraft of other times; it is also true that sex plays no small part in the activities of certain occult groups today. But by and large three factors inhibit the modern witch in the pursuit of un-licensed sexual excess. Firstly, few people are strikingly beautiful in the nude, and modern witches are no exception. Pot bellies and dangling breasts are far more common than lithe young limbs where 'wicca' is con-cerned. Secondly a great deal of whirling and dancing goes on at the average coven meeting, leading to a state of almost total exhaustion – which has a bearing on the third point: a good ninety per cent of modern witches are past their prime, being sedentary workers in the late thirties and forties. One former coven member told me: 'The object of dancing around, originally, was to work up excitement and sexual energy which, unin-hibited by clothing, projected an almost tangible emo-tional sensation which the witches call the "cone of power". In fact I have scarcely ever seen a male witch with an erection after such a communal dance.'

As will be seen in a later chapter, ritual flagellation and sexual intercourse are both included in some rites of the 'wicca'. But mass orgies are not. In fact with its element of voyeurism and mild sexual titillation, modern witchcraft appeals to those people whose flag-ging sexual energies need a booster, rather than the insatiable satyrs conjured up by Sunday newspaper reports.

In any case, witches rarely thrust their sexual atten-tions on any outsider, just as they refrain from pushing their religious views. But modern witchcraft, like any other emotive concern, has been exploited by the unscrupulous. So-called 'black magic' groups, who persuade newcomers to take off their clothes and indulge in all kinds of grotesque sexual activity, secretly photograph them, and then use the photographs for blackmail, are not unknown in most large cities. Again prostitution, either covert or overt, is often the purpose of magic-cum-witchcraft circles. For the great advantage of ritual is, of course, that it can take many forms – any perverted but imaginative mind could invent ceremonies which involved either male or female homosexuality, sado-masochism, mass copulation and so on, while cloaking the whole thing in a quasi-mystical veil of mumbo-jumbo which would tend to uninhibit those too nervous to resort to a whore in the ordinary way. London has few of these groups nowadays, though both London and Birmingham apparently had their fair share of such outfits just after the war. Today they thrive mainly in the Pigalle districts of Paris, the red-light districts of Hamburg and West Berlin, and various parts of New York, and beside them the British witch-cult looks rather tame.

This then, is the typical modern British witch: nearing middle age, lower middle class, mildly frustrated sexually. To them all, witchcraft stands in the place of more orthodox religion, and it is hard, speaking to them, to doubt that they sincerely believe this. They claim that they are the direct, linear descendants of the witches executed during the Middle Ages and that, though driven underground, their cult survived throughout the centuries. In fact, 'wicca' is extremely difficult to trace back further than 1949. In that year a novel purporting to give a true account of what witches believe appeared under the title *High Magic's Aid*. Its author was an extraordinary man named Gerald Brosseau Gardner.

3

Gerald Gardner

ON the early morning of February 12, 1964, a frail old man with a goatee beard and strangely piercing eyes collapsed and died in the breakfast lounge of the SS *Scottish Prince*, a passenger vessel which was steaming slowly along the coast of North Africa. Gerald Brosseau Gardner was eighty years old at the time of his death; and he was acclaimed by the Press as 'King of the British Witches'.

Because of his bizarre claim to fame Gardner's death caused a minor stir in newspapers all over the world. He had boarded the ship at Beirut, after wintering in the Lebanon, and after formalities had been carried out he was buried at Tunis, the next port of call. But even his funeral did not mark the end of the Gardner story, for the publication of his will, signed only a month before his death, sparked off an unholy wrangle among Britain's remaining witches as to who should inherit his arbitrary 'title'.

The question of whether Gardner himself had in any way deserved the title 'Witch King' was one which interested observers of the argument; certainly the old man had secretly revelled in the notoriety which it brought him, and the publicity which it gave to his museum of witchcraft on the Isle of Man. It was also true that the particular cult referred to as 'modern witchcraft' owed much of its popularity to the books which Gardner had written about it. But the principal point at issue with folklorists was: did Gardner 'invent' modern witchcraft, or the 'Wicca' as he called it; or did he – as he claimed – discover an hereditary cult in Britain which was older than Christianity?

Gardner had a curious childhood for a man later destined to be leader of a witch-cult; in fact it was a curious childhood altogether. He was born on June 13, 1884, at Great Crosby, Lancashire, where his father William Robert Gardner was a wealthy timber merchant. The house in which he lived until he was seven stood on a wooded stretch overlooking the sea, and frequently echoed to the sound of Gardner's brother shooting at birds from an upper storey with a Martini-Henry rifle. Across the road lived Gardner's Uncle Joe, a rich religious maniac who hated 'Papists' and alternated between membership of the Methodists and the Anglicans, building churches for both of them. William Gardner himself had several curious habits, one of the oddest being that at the slightest sign of rain he would take off his clothes, fold them neatly, and sit, naked, upon them until the shower was over.

It was in such surroundings that Gardner, an asthmatic child, lived until he was seven, when he was sent abroad for the first time in the care of a buxom Irish nannie named Josephine McCombie, known as

'Com'. 'Com' was a kind girl at heart, although she liked whisky and men in about equal proportions, and tended to beat young Gerald if he interfered too much with the pursuit of either interest. Together 'Com' and Gerald travelled in the Canary Islands and North Africa, 'Com' collecting admirers, and Gardner collecting daggers and knives while at the same time teaching himself to read with the aid of the *Strand Magazine.*

In 1900, when Gardner was sixteen, 'Com' finally married a wealthy tea planter from Ceylon, and when she sailed for Colombo, Gardner sailed with her to begin a new life in the East. From then until his retirement and return to England in 1936, Gardner followed several pursuits in several countries – he became a rubber planter, a customs officer, and an amateur archaeologist and weapons expert, and lived at various times in Ceylon, Malaya, and Borneo.

It was while in the East that his early interest in mysticism and the occult grew and was fostered by native 'spiritualist' practices and customs. Once, while on leave in England in 1927, Gardner decided to investigate 'Western spiritualism' and when he married his wife Donna in that same year, he convinced himself that the spirits had foretold their marriage. Later he visited Cyprus, and became certain that he had been a sword maker there in a previous incarnation.

Superficially, the facts of Gardner's life after his retirement and return to England in 1936 are relatively simple. In Malaya, he had become interested in the history and evolution of the Malay *kris,* a sort of curly bladed dagger, and wrote a pamphlet on the subject entitled *Keris and other Malay Weapons*. In 1939, perhaps with memories of his father's peculiarity when confronted with rain, he took up nudism, convinced that it had definite therapeutic powers, and in March of the same year joined the Folk Lore Society. He marked the occasion of his inauguration with an address to the Society on a box of 'witch relics' in his possession, alleged to have belonged to Matthew Hopkins, the 17th-century 'Witchfinder General'.

Gardner's relationship with the Folk Lore Society continued unbroken until his death – he was a member, from March 1946, of the Council of the Society, and he contributed to the Society's journal *Folk Lore* on such subjects as 'Hazel as a Weapon' and charms, amulets, and talismans.

In the same year as he joined the Folk Lore Society, Gardner joined another organisation whose headquarters were close to his home in Christchurch, Hampshire, in the New Forest. It was his first witch-coven, and according to Gardner it was led by a lady who lived in a big house and went by the name of 'Old Dorothy'. Old Dorothy convinced Gardner, according to his book *Witchcraft Today*, published in 1954, that witchcraft, or 'The Wicca' was the survival of an ancient, pre-Christian fertility cult, the Old Religion of Britain.

In 1949, under the pen name 'Scire', Gardner published a novel entitled *High Magic's Aid* which purported to give authentic details of witchcraft in the Middle Ages, and with the repeal of the Witchcraft

Act in 1951, he saw fit to publish his two factual books on the subject, *Witchcraft Today* and *The Meaning of Witchcraft* (1959). In the meantime, he had bought a ruined windmill and its outbuildings at Castletown, in the Isle of Man, from Cecil H. Williamson, who had founded a witchcraft museum there in the forties, and who currently runs a similar museum in Boscastle, Cornwall. To Williamson's museum exhibits, Gardner added some of his own, including his by-now extensive weapon collection, and it was in Castletown that his wife died in 1960, four years before her husband. When Gardner's will was published, it was discovered that his property in Castletown, plus his personal estate, was in excess of £20,000. The museum, the collection, and a portion of other property was willed to Mrs Monique Wilson, who along with her husband runs the museum at Castletown today. The rest of Gardner's money went to a few remaining relatives and to several of the 'witches' initiated by him, including Jack L. Bracelin, co-founder with Gardner of a nudist colony in St Alban's and the biographer of the 'chief witch'.

To many people who adhered to his witchcraft beliefs, Gardner was a 'learned old man', a 'brilliant scholar', and a much maligned individual. Bracelin's book *Gerald Gardner: Witch*, published in 1960 by the Octagon Press, amounts almost to a hagiography.

Unfortunately for the Gardnerians, there are several facts which seem to indicate that, to put it mildly, Gardner was less than honest in his dealings.

To begin with, there is the fact that the membership

list of the Folk Lore Society for November 1950 suddenly describes him as holding the degrees of M.A.
and Ph.D. while in the first edition, 1963, of *Author's
and Writer's Who's Who* he is described as 'Ph.D.,
D.Litt.' In the next sentence, he is said to have been
educated 'privately'. In fact he admitted to Bracelin
that he taught himself to read, and there is no record
of his having attended even a kindergarten, let alone
a university. The degrees were apparently not hono-
rary, so that, to interpret the situation as kindly as
possible, we must assume that Gardner worked extremely hard in the late fifties to obtain extra-mural
degrees from some unnamed university and that, with
commendable modesty, he mentioned his studies to
no one.

However, Gardner does not appear to have been a
particularly modest man. One of his former witchcraft
colleagues describes him as being a 'tremendous snob'
and certainly he took great pride in claiming distant
descent from Baron Gardner of Uttoxeter, the former
Admiral and Commander in Chief of the Channel
Fleet during the Napoleonic Wars.

Another ancestor whom he claimed – impressing his
followers – was Grizell Gairdner, burned as a witch at
Newburgh, Scotland, in 1640, and Bracelin's biography
contains an appendix which lists Gerald's ancestors,
tracing his lineage rather shakily back to one Simon
Le Gardinor of 1379.

On occasion Gardner wore a kilt, and in his will he
left to a sister-in-law 'My grandfather's Dirk, my grandfather's Skign Dhoo [stocking knife], my kilt with all

its belongings, my plaid with its brooch, my grandfather's sword with its cross belt [known as the Rhyming Sword]'.

What of Gardner's scholarship? Certainly he was a dilettante whose interest stretched from amateur archaeology in Johore to the evolution of the modern Service revolver, and his arms collection on the Isle of Man is vast. But on occasion, his enthusiasms seem to have led him into dishonesty.

Stewart Sanderson, M.A., Director of the Institute of Dialect and Folk Life Studies at Leeds University remembers his only contact with Gardner at the International Congress on Maritime Folklore and Ethnology held at Naples in 1954.

Describing him as 'that strange man Gardner', Mr Sanderson recalls: 'He appeared with his wife; wore an extraordinary copper snake bangle on one wrist, and one day I actually saw a fisherman on the Lungomare make the cornuto sign against the evil eye as Gardner crossed over from the tram stop.'

Gardner read a paper which was later published in the proceedings of the Congress. Its subject was the development of Manx fishing craft, and on the surface it was a scholarly piece of research.

'However,' says Mr Sanderson, 'the article gave no references and no acknowledgments were made to earlier studies of the subject. It is, in fact, a scissors and paste job with a sprinkling of folk lore beliefs at the end, based on Basil and Eleanor Mewgaw, "The Development of the Manx Fishing Craft", in Proceedings of the Isle of Man Natural History and Antiquarian Society, 1952, and also on an article in *Mariner's Mirror*, April 1941.'

It is perhaps significant that, though he had been a member of its council for eighteen years, the Folk Lore Society did not publish Gardner's obituary in its journal. One reason for this is hinted at by the journal's editor, Christina Hole, who is herself a leading folklorist and author. In a letter to *Man, Myth and Magic* Miss Hole writes:

Dr Gardner had a very curious personality. It did not inspire confidence – at least not in me, nor in a number of people interested in witchcraft and kindred matters. His theories were in themselves somewhat peculiar. I remember a meeting when the composition of the Council for the following year was discussed, and the question was raised as to whether his presence on our Council was really advantageous to the Society. Nothing was done about it, and his name was allowed to go forward as before, but the doubt was clearly felt and expressed.

The national Press also expressed doubt about Gardner's theories. Both his non-fiction books on witchcraft, in fact, are obviously derived from the works of Eliphas Lévi, McGregor Mathers, Aleister Crowley, and the anthropologist Dr Margaret Murray, with a leavening of bits from the known portions of the mysteries of Eleusis, from records of witchcraft trials, from theories first propounded by Montague Summers, and from G. E. Leland's *Aradia* – a book of Tuscan witchcraft, published in the late 19th century.

In his books, Gardner barely hinted at sexual rites,

and strove to achieve general acceptance by insisting that witchcraft was a religion to be respected like any other. In fact, Gardnerian witchcraft involved a good deal of sexual contact, including ritual flagellation and nudity. To describe his rituals on paper, Gardner used a sort of shorthand consisting of one letter symbols; the 'five fold kiss', during which the High Priestess kisses her High Priest on the lips, breasts, and genitals was signified by a capital 'S' while flagellation was signified by a capital 'S' with an oblique stroke running through it, rather like a dollar sign.

'Gardnerian' groups today can be fairly easily spotted by their rituals and their equipment, although some at least have dropped the more blatantly sexual rituals, such as Gardner's 'Great Rite' – sexual intercourse between priest and priestess in front of the assembled coven.

One of the 'giveaways' of Gardnerian cults is their use of the 'athame' or black handled knife. Gardner claimed that this was the traditional witch's weapon, to be carried at all times. In fact the only reference to an 'athame' in occult writings of 'pre-Gardner' days appears to be that in the 'Key of Solomon' grimoire. Here, the word is spelt 'arthame' and is described as being the knife with which the magician outlines his magic circle. It is perhaps significant that the plates showing how to make an 'arthame' have been torn from the McGregor Mathers translation of the 'Key of Solomon' in the British Museum.

It is tempting to speculate on whether Gardner's early beatings at the hands of the voluptuous 'Com' had anything to do with his later preoccupation with ritual flagellation. In any case, we are still faced with the original question – did Gardner invent modern witchcraft or was he, under all his trappings, genuine?

Perhaps Gardner carried the secret to the grave with him. The unassailable facts are, however, that although 'village wise women' skilled in the art of herbal medicine have certainly existed for centuries in various parts of Britain, all of them have tended to be lone operators. Apart from the records of witch trials, there is little independent evidence of witch 'cults' ever having been widespread in England. Even the assiduous hunter of esoteric folk lore, G. E. Leland – whose book *Aradia* has been mentioned previously – makes no mention of a pagan witch cult. Leland's notes at the British Museum are a mine of odd information – gypsy methods of making glue, herbal medicine in Ireland, and so on. But nowhere does he mention anything like the cults described by Gardner as having existed in such profusion throughout the 18th- and 19th-century British countryside. Bearing in mind Leland's deep interest in Tuscan witch-lore, we can take it for granted that he searched very earnestly in his own country for similar phenomena: his records show that he found none.

4

Early Witchcraft

ALTHOUGH Gardner's 'wicca' is readily seen, on close examination, to be derived from the sources mentioned in the previous chapter, he was perfectly correct when he said that witches in one form or another had existed since 'time immemorial'. There seems to have been no time or place on earth where witchcraft and magic have not been practised. Man's attempt to change exterior natural phenomena by the application of secret formulae through ritual and ceremonial is an essential part of his way of thinking and behaving.

It is customary to trace the origins of witchcraft and ceremonial magic as we know it to the Akkadean-Chaldean inscriptions of Nineveh in the second millenium BC, but this is simply a question of the survival of written texts. The invocations are already highly sophisticated and suggest a long tradition of magic practice:

They are seven! They are seven!
In the depths of the ocean they are seven!
In the brilliancy of the heavens they are seven!
They proceed from the ocean depths, from the hidden re-

treat. They are neither male nor female, those which stretch themselves out like chains, they have no spouse, they do not produce children; they are strangers to benevolence.

Before the Akkadean texts we have only the evidence of primitive sculpture and cave painting which suggest the eternal preoccupations of magic: fertility, rain-making, success in hunting, the warding off of sickness or misfortune or of evil spirits. Magic was a necessary element in everyday life. Art, religion, and magic are inextricably interwoven with each other. As Montague Summers put it: 'The reason why man "came forth believing in terrors and evils" is simply that terrors and evils were there and very real and the simplicity of primitive man was sensibly conscious of their activities and of their presence all about him.' Nineveh seems to have shared our own confusion between the operation of black and white magic. Their religious system appears to have been dualist but the two elements were so intermingled as to result in what Butler, in *Ritual Magic*, termed 'an extremely elaborate and well-developed demonology'.

The Magician has bewitched me with his magic, he has
    bewitched me with his magic;
He who has fashioned images corresponding to my whole
    appearance has bewitched my whole appearance;
He has seized the magic draught prepared for me and has
    soiled my garments;
He has torn my garments and has mingled his magic herb
    with the dust of my feet;
May the fire-God, the hero, turn their magic to naught!

It is all there. We might be in Salem or Pendle Forest. Man is already fashioning wax-images to destroy his enemy. The two streams of magic are already clearly defined: the thaumaturgic spells and petty incantations of primitive witchcraft which were the acquired knowledge of any wise woman from Nineveh to Chelmsford, and the highly complex and demanding rituals of ceremonial magic binding angels and demons to do one's bidding.

> The wicked God, the wicked Demon,
> The demon of the desert, the demon of the mountain,
> The demon of the sea, the demon of the marsh,
> Spirit of the heavens, conjure it!
> Spirit of the earth, conjure it!

It is not long before we find the civil authorities hot on the trail of witchcraft. Hammurabi seems to have had to legislate for the Matthew Hopkinses of his community: 'If a man has laid a charge of witchcraft on another man and has not justified it, he upon whom the witchcraft charge is laid shall go to the holy river, and if the holy river overcome him, he who accused him shall take to himself his house.' The rules are rather different from 17th-century East-Anglian witch-floating, but the instinct is the same. There are instances of the death penalty for witchcraft in 19th-dynasty Egypt, and in Assyria. There seems to have been no time when the practice of the black arts could be carried out without fear.

Between Nineveh and Babylon, between the Graeco Egyptians and the Kabbalah it is possible to argue a continuity of method and belief. Some of this may be mere coincidence but there seems little doubt that the rituals were passed on and refashioned. They certainly became more complicated: 'When the sun's disc is clear above the horizon, decapitate an immaculate, pure white cock, holding it in the crook of your left elbow; circumnambulate the altar before sunrise. . . . Throw the head into the river, catch the blood in your right hand and drink it.' But the aims were much the same: 'Let her sleep with none other, let her have no pleasurable intercourse with any other man save me. Let her neither drink nor eat, nor love, nor be strong, nor well, let her have not sleep except with me.'

Much has been written of the witchcraft references in the Bible. At the height of the witch craze they were used without question to justify torture and persecution and burning. 'A man also or a woman that hath a familiar spirit or that is a wizard, shall surely be put to death; they shall stone them with stones: their blood shall be upon them' (Lev, XX, 27). But many of the texts are more ambiguous. As early as 1584 Reginald Scot, in his *Discovery of Witchcraft*, pointed out that the most notorious text of all – 'Thou shalt not suffer a witch to live' – should be translated – 'You shall not suffer any poisoners to live.'

There is no evidence at all in the Bible for witchcraft as an organised religion. As Walter Scott wrote: 'It cannot be said that in any part of that sacred volume, a text occurs indicating the system of witchcraft, under the Jewish dispensation, in any respect similar to that against which the law books of so many European nations have, till very lately, denounced punishment.'

The fullest account of witchcraft in the Bible is that of Saul's visit to the witch of Endor. Saul had suppressed 'all those that had familiar spirits and wizards' but, feeling considerable misgivings about his forthcoming battle with the Philistines and getting no response from God, he sought 'a woman that had a familiar spirit' and asked her to summon up Samuel from the Dead. The necromantic rite is not described. The woman saw 'gods ascending out of the earth', Samuel appears and warns Saul of disaster. The whole episode has considerable power and conviction. It is matched by many other instances of necromancy in European and middle eastern literature. What is difficult to establish is how far these reflect real practice of divination by attempting to raise the dead. It may simply be that this is the kind of scene that every good epic should have. In the Sumerian Epic of Gilgamish the hero raises from the dead the spirit of his friend Enkidu. Aeschylus gives a vivid account of the raising from the dead of Darius in his play *The Persians*.

Milk, sweet and white, from an unblemished cow; the
     gleam of
flower-confected honey; lustral water, drawn
From virgin springs; and from the fields, this unmixed
     draught,
The quickening essence of its ancient parent vine;
Here too is fragrant oil from the pale olive, which
Thrives in perpetual leaf; and last, these garlands, twined

With flowers, the children of the all producing earth.
So, friends, assist now this libation to the dead;
With solemn chants summon Darius from his grave ...

The details are so wholly different from any other
necromantic rite that one is tempted to dismiss this as
the imagination of the poet, but we know that Aeschylus was, at one stage in his life, prosecuted for giving
away the secrets of the Eleusinian rites, so that he
must, to some extent, have been writing from the
inside.

A very different, if more conventional, picture of
necromantic ritual is given by Homer in the ninth
book of the Odyssey:

When I had finished my prayers and invocations to the
communities of the dead, I took the sheep and cut their
throats over the trench so that the dark blood flowed in.
And now the souls of the dead who had gone below came
swarming up from Erebus. . . . From this multitude of souls
as they fluttered to and fro by the trench, there came a
moaning that was pitiful to hear. Panic drained the blood
from my cheeks.

Undoubtedly it was Homer's lurid description that
most influenced the writers of classical Rome. But in
Rome we are on firmer ground. We sense that there is
a great deal of solid reality behind the literary ritual
invocations. There is a strong feeling of sordid prac-
ticality about witchcraft rather like that of the Paris
of Louis XIV. 'Magic,' wrote Apuleius, who certainly
knew what he was talking about, 'is secretive and foul
and horrible, usually practised at night and shrouded

in darkness.' When Germanicus was dying, by poisoning he suspected, Tacitus tells us that: 'Examination of the floor and walls of his bedroom revealed the remains of human bodies, spells, curses, lead tablets inscribed with the patient's name, charred and bloody ashes, and other malignant objects which are supposed to consign souls to the powers of the tomb' (*Annals*, 2, 69). Caligula, according to Suetonius, was 'believed to have drunk a love philtre administered by his wife Caesonia and been driven mad'. Love philtres seem to have been in fantastic demand in ancient Rome and witchcraft must have been a thriving industry. Apuleius quotes a recipe for an aphrodisiac: 'pills and nails and threads, roots and herbs and shoots, the two tailed lizard and charms from mares'. In the *Satyricon* of Petronius, Polyaenos seeks the aid of a witch to cure his temporarily diminished virility with remarkable results:

At the conclusion of her incantations, she commanded me to spit three times. Next she handed me some pebbles, each of which had been individually charmed and wrapped in purple cloth, and told me to drop them down my crotch. Then she reached in with hand to see what response, if any, she had awakened. And lo, pat to her spells, that ghostly part of me obeyed, inching and lurching into enormous life until it quite filled her hand. 'Oh Chrysis,' she gasped delightedly, 'just look at the hare I've started for the hunters.'

Witchcraft is a positive obsession with the poets of Rome, and one can only draw the conclusion that it was a similar obsession in daily life. In almost every case the witch is consulted or employed for help in a love affair. Here is a witch from Tibullus:

Her have I known the stars of heaven to charm,
The rapid river's course by spells to turn,
Cleave graves, bid bones descend from pyres still warm,
Or coax the manes forth from silent urn.
Hell's rabble now she calls with magic scream,
Now bids them milk-sprent to their homes below:
At will lights cloudy skies with sunshine's gleam,
At will 'neath summer orbs collects the snow.

Elegies, 2

and another from Horace:

Candia with dishevell'd hair
And short crisp vipers coiling there,
Besides a fire of Colchos stands,
And her attendant hag commands
To feed the flames with fig trees torn
From dead men's sepulchres forlorn,
With dismal cypress, eggs rubbed o'er
With filthy toads' envenomed gore.

Satires, 2

Girls in Virgil's eclogues perform rites to bring back lovers, there are witches in Ovid, and in Plautus; Pliny is fascinated by the subject, Apuleius obsessed by it. It was left to Lucan to have the last word on the subject. In the *Pharsalia* he gives us Ericthe – the witch to end all witches:

Leanness has possession of the features of the hag, foul with filthiness, and, unknown to a clear sky, her dreadful visage, laden with uncombed locks, is beset with

Stygian paleness. The seeds she treads on of the fruitful
corn she burns up and by her breathing makes air noxious
that was not deadly before.

The situation is similar to that of Saul consulting the
witch of Endor. Pompey wishes to know the result of
the next day's battle, and seeks out Erictho to reveal
the future for him by necromancy. They crawl by night
over the field of the previous day's fighting seeking out
a corpse whose lungs are still intact. She finds a suitable
vehicle. 'Then in the first place does she fill his breast,
opened by fresh wounds with reeking blood, and she
bathes his marrow with gore, and plentifully supplies
venom from the moon. Here is mingled whatever, by
a monstrous generation, nature has produced.' The list
includes dogs' foam, the entrails of a lynx, hyena drop-
pings, the marrow of a stag that has fed on serpents,
the eyes of dragons and the slough of the horned ser-
pent of Lybya. The body slowly begins to take on a
new life: 'The eyes with their apertures distended
wide are opened. In it not as yet is there the face of
one living, but of one now dying. His paleness and
stiffness remain, and, brought back to the world, he is
astounded. But his sealed lips resound with no mur-
mur. A voice and a tongue to answer alone are granted
him.'

Like Samuel the soldier prophesies disaster. The
corpse is burned as a reward for his services so that he
will not be disturbed in a like manner again.

How far this is literary artifice, how far a heightened
version of magic practice it is impossible to conclude.

Necromancy through the centuries has followed a ritual very similar to that carried out by Erictho. John Weever writes of the 16th-century sorcerer Edmund Kelley:

The black ceremonies of the night being ended, Kelley demanded of one of the gentleman's servants what corpse was the last buried in Law churchyard, who told him of a poor man that was buried there but the same day. He and the said Waring entreated this foresaid servant to go with them to the grave of the man so lately interred, which he did; and withal did help them to dig up the carcase of the poor caitiff, whom by their incantations they made him (or some evil spirit through his organs) to speak, who delivered strange predictions concerning the said gentleman.

Rome offers us the fullest survey of witchcraft in action that we are to find for many years. What is not clear is how far witchcraft is an organised communal activity. The general impression to be gained from what evidence there is is that of the witch working alone. There is a communal body of lore and many similarities in practice, but as in Israel there is no evidence that witchcraft ever took on the status of an organised underground religion. The situation is confused by the omniverousness of the Roman attitude towards religion. There is considerable evidence of the cult of the celtic God Cernunnos, but nothing to suggest, as Margaret Murray does, that he was the God of the witches. Lucan refers to the worship of Teutates, Esus, and Taranis by sacrifice of drowning, burning, and hanging but there is nothing to suggest that this was more than a sporadic cult activity. As for ceremonial magic, the path from Babylon seems to continue uninterrupted, but channelled into formalised religious activity. Apuleius writes in *De Magia*: 'If, as I read among very many writers, what the Persians call magician is what we call priest, what crime is it, I ask you, to be a magician and to have a thorough knowledge and understanding and skill in the laws of ceremonials, the proper form of sacred rites, the ordinances of religious practices?'

Nevertheless magicians were punished in Rome with great severity. Tacitus relates how Lucius Pituanius was hurled from the Tarpeian Rock and how Publius Marcius was stripped and lashed to death outside the Esquiline gate. Constantine carried on a determined warfare against the black arts but made provision for white witchcraft as a cure for diseases and as a means of preventing hail and storms destroying the crops.

With the break-up of the Roman empire our sources of information, both literary and actual, begin to dry up. That the practice both of witchcraft and ceremonial magic was continued is certain, but in what form and with what degree of intensity we have no way of telling. Only the codes of law that have survived make it clear that the problem was a never-ending one. For the most part these consist of practicable laws and decrees punishing witchcraft with summary death or banishment. Occasionally attempts were made to approach the problem rationally. The Lombards with remarkable sense of proportion expressly forbade the burning of witches since the crimes of which they were accused were manifestly impossible. A Saxon law is equally reasonable: 'If anyone be found that shall henceforth practice any heathenship or in any way love witchcraft let him pay ten half marks; half to Christ, half to the king.' A law of Athelstan punishes witchcraft, even where death is involved, by one hundred and twenty days in prison. We should remember, however, that many of the laws of this time were remarkable for their mildness. Consider this law of the City of Chester: he who was guilty of robbery or theft or assaulted a woman in a house, paid a fine of forty shillings. A maker of bad beer paid four shillings.

But as Christianity gathered strength and confidence the laws became more severe. Edgar in 959 forbade 'well worshippings and necromancies and divinations' and enjoined that on feast days 'heathen songs and devil's games be abstained from'. The punishment for disobeying this ordinance was death. At this time there is a great risk of confusing the lingering traces of the old religion with the pursuit of witchcraft. Many still clung determinedly to their old Gods or worshipped them in secret, but this is something very distinct from witchcraft or sorcery. They seem utterly distinct from any kind of religious activity without constituting in themselves a religion.

Magic is a specialist activity – a kind of branch of primitive science – and not a religion. William the Conqueror at the siege of Ely in 1071 makes use of a witch rather as he would make use of miner or a pioneer:

He sent for a witch, who was to disconcert by her magic all the warlike devices of the Saxons. The magician was placed in a wooden tower at the head of the works in progress, but at the moment when the soldiers and pioneers were confidently advancing, Hereward sallied out from the side, and firing the forest of osiers which covered the marsh, destroyed in the flames the sorceress and most of the soldiers and Norman workmen who were with her.

Thierry, *The Norman Conquest*, 1, 267

The spells of the Saxons are charming, poetical and very much bound up with the daily life and observations of the common people:

Wen, wen, little wen,
Here thou shalt not build, nor have any abode.
But thou must pass forth to the hill hard by,
Where thou hast a brother in misery.
He shall lay a leaf at thy head.
Under the foot of the wolf, under the wing of the eagle,
ever mayest thou fade.
Shrivel as coal on the hearth,
Shrink as muck in the wall
And waste away like water in a bucket.

There is no question of harnessing dark forces, only the furtherance of a primitive form of sympathetic magic. There is certainly no hint of a pact with the powers of evil.

The hardening of witchcraft into Satanism is essentially bound up with the changing attitude of the Church towards the existence of evil. It may be too strong to say that the religion of witchcraft was devised by the Church for its own ends, but it certainly gave a

strong lead. Satan grew up to be an all powerful force
in the religion of the middle ages because the Church
needed him to be so. The origins of the problem have
been set out with great clarity by Runciman in *The
Medieval Manichee*:

Sin was a very real thing to the early christians. The world
that they knew, the cruel luxurious, uncertain world of
the Roman Empire, was undoubtedly a wicked place. How
had such wickedness come into creation? If God was the
Creator and God was omnipotent and good, why did he
permit such things to be? The Fall might explain why
man was enchained in sin, but the Fall could not create
sin; rather it was sin that created the fall.

For the Manicheans and the many similar heretical
sects the solution lay in some kind of dualism in which
the powers of good and evil were arrayed in eternal
conflict, but for the Church it was unthinkable that
God and Satan should be co-equals. Satan had to
operate within the permission afforded him by God.
But once the Church had satisfied itself on this tech-
nicality mankind became the centre of a Holy War.
God could always withdraw his permission for the
operation of the Devil, but while it still held, the Devil
was the enemy.

The Devil is both the enemy and the avenger of God. The
enemy when he seems to love us and to seduce us to prefer
momentary bliss to eternal, and makes us the enemies of
the Creator. The avenger, when he asks our punishment
because through sin we have made ourselves his slaves. . . .
When permitted, he comes like a whirlwind cruelly against

those over whom God lets him have power, not that he desires to fulfil the divine command, but because he seeks to gratify his special hatred against us.

Maximus, 662

The great difficulty is to trace by what stages and on what level of reality witchcraft became the religion of Satan. For liberal historians, from Lea to Trevor Roper, there is no question about the matter at all. Witchcraft was the invention of the Inquisitors, the torturers, the Prince Bishops, and the witch finders. For Margaret Murray the witchcraft of the middle ages was but one phase of 'a continuity of belief and ritual which can be traced from the Palaeological period down to modern times'. What seems possible, however, is that as the Church made the Devil more and more a factor of daily life; man began to seek him out as a refuge and as a consolation. If it were really within his power to give limitless happiness on earth and power over all things, if his cult was life giving and life enhancing, if he was worshipped with feasting and drinking and debauchery, why should not man, in the midst of so much physical misery and deprivation and confronted with a church which taught only a remote bliss in a life to come which could be achieved only by abstinence and self discipline, worship Satan in preference to God. Moreover, the early middle ages were full of folk tales and legends of men who had sought out the help of the Devil for building bridges or obtaining the love of a girl who had despised them, and who at the last moment had cheated him of their souls either through their own shrewd cunning or the

intervention of the saints or the Blessed Virgin. The
risk must have seemed one well worth taking. Michelet,
who subscribed whole-heartedly to this point of a view,
paints a vivid, if somewhat tuppence-coloured picture
of a woman's conversion to the religion of Satan.

Oh, miserable Saints of wood, of what avail to make vows
to them? Are they deaf? or are they grown old? Why have
I not a Spirit to protect me, strong and powerful – if an
evil Spirit, I cannot help it? I see them many a one carved
on the church door. . . . Oh for strength and power! Who
can give me those? I would gladly give my whole self in
exchange. . .

The Church was slow to act against witchcraft. What
decrees were passed during the first millennium are
secular rather than religious. The laws of Charlemagne
punish with death those who work with the devil to
raise tempests, while at the same time prescribing the
death penalty for mob burnings of witches. But there
is no indication of any organised attack on the powers
of evil. It is not until the Church's first thousand years
have passed that it seems sufficiently assured to root out
heresies with fire and sword. A new energy seems to
possess the Christian world. This finds expression in
Urban's preaching of the First Crusade in Clermont in
1095, but it equally finds expression in its hideous consequence – the massacre of the Jews of Mainz and
Cologne in the following year. It was not until the
impulse of the crusades had begun to die away that the
Church began to put its own house in order and when
it did so it was with great determination and ferocity.

5

The Persecution

THE Inquisition was founded in 1163 by the Council of Tours. Its aim was to strengthen and fortify an ailing church, to drive out immorality and weakness from within and to exterminate heresy without. It was given into the hands of the Dominicans who rapidly earned themselves the formidable nickname *'domini canes'* – 'the hounds of the Lord'. Their first aim was to root out the Manichean heresy in any form it might be found. Any religious system that posed a dualist solution to the problem of evil was anathema to the church. The Waldensians were denounced in 1184 and were accused, among other things, of worshipping the devil, riding broomsticks, and cannibalism. In 1209 a Bull of Innocent III launched the Albigensian crusade against the Cathars. The essential purity of their faith was distorted into detailed and grotesque accounts of their intercourse with the devil. In 1307 the highest military order in the church, the Knights Templar, was declared anathema and destroyed. The Templars were accused of worshipping an idol named Baphomet, of trampling on the Cross, of homosexuality. But by this time the witches themselves had come under the scourge of the Inquisition.

The first person technically to be burned as a witch was a woman of Toulouse, Angéle de Labarthe, convicted of intercourse with the devil in 1275, but a good deal of ground work had been put in before then. Writers like Caesarius von Heisterbach had attributed to the devil, thunderstorms, hail storms, diseases, floods, unexpected noises, and the rustling of the wind. William of Paris had asserted that juggling was so complex an art that it could only be performed with the aid of demons. The great Thomas Aquinas had written: 'Witchcraft is so enduring that it permits of no remedy by human operation', and in his commentary on the Book of Job had brooded deeply on the problem of intercourse with the devil: 'Because the incubus demon is able to steal the semen of an innocent youth in nocturnal emissions and pour it into the womb of a woman, she is able by this semen to conceive an offspring whose father is not the demon incubus, but the man whose semen impregnated her, because it took effect by the virtue of him from whom it was dissipated. Therefore it seems that a man is able, without a miracle, to be at one and the same time, both a virgin and a father.'

In 1227 Pope Gregory VII sent Conrad of Marburg on a mission to Germany with unlimited powers to bring to the stake a sect of Satanists. This is the first instance of a fully organised witchhunt in Europe and it set patterns that later generations were to follow. There had been rumours of Luciferans who worshipped Satan, kissed the backsides of toads and cats, and indulged in indiscriminate orgies. Conrad was a lunatic sadist who had been confessor to Elizabeth of Thuringia. He had forced on her a series of indecent and humiliating corporal punishments in consequence of which the poor woman was canonised. He pursued his hunt for Satanists with equal fervour and soon had a formidable list of confessions. The German clergy protested against him in vain. The Archbishop of Mayence wrote to the Pope:

Whoever fell into his hands, had only the choice between a ready confession for the sake of saving his life and a denial, whereupon he was speedily burnt. Every false witness was accepted, but no just defence granted – not even to people of prominence. The person arraigned had to confess that he was a heretic, that he had touched a toad, that he had kissed a pale man, or some monster. Many catholics suffered themselves to be burnt instantly rather than confess to such vicious crimes, of which they knew they were not guilty.

In 1233 Conrad overstepped himself. He denounced a nobleman, Count Henry of Sayn, and was murdered by his followers. He, too, was subsequently canonised.

In 1234 an army led by the Duke of Brabant crushed with considerable thoroughness and ferocity the Stedingers – a large tribe of Frisian peasants who went on the rampage. The terms in which they were condemned by the Papacy show how far Satanism had become a convenient label to attach to any form of rebellion.

Seduced by Satan, they have abjured all laws, human and divine; they have derided the Church, insulted and horribly profaned the Sacraments; consulted with witches to raise evil spirits; shed innocent blood like water; burned and blundered and destroyed; they are in fine enemies to all good, having concocted an infernal scheme to propagate the cult of the devil, whom they adore and their secret Sabbaths.

Because of the thoroughness with which the persecutions were carried out it is virtually impossible to glimpse what reality, if any, lay behind them. It is possible that Cathar extremists went in for Satanic orgies, but is more likely that this is simply a distortion of the vital role that Satan played in the Manichean cosmos. It is possible that there was some hidden mystery within the religion of the Knights Templar, but the ferocity with which they were destroyed and the relentless repetition of the confessions extracted from them by torture suggest that they had been judged and condemned long before the trials began. A penurious king envied their power and needed their wealth. A subservient pope was only too willing to lend his support to a persecution that would remove for ever a separate religious power within his own church. Since, as far as we can tell, the questions of the torturers were all of the 'When did you stop beating your wife?' category the unanimity of the confessions is not surprising.

As for the Luciferans they present the kind of problem that confronts us over and over again in trying to distinguish between fact and fantasy in witchcraft. It

seems probable that there were sects practising Satanism, but fanatics like Conrad were all too quick to
believe that they were fighting in a struggle where all
mankind had gone over to the devil, and if the Archbishop of Mayence is to be believed he created what he
set out to destroy.

From this point onwards the methods of trying and
condemning witches have nothing to do with the pro-
cesses of ordinary law. Accusation itself is sufficient
proof. Boniface VIII summed up the situation with
stark brutality. Those accused of witchcraft were to be
dealt with 'simply and squarely, without the noise and
form of lawyers and judges'.

There remained the problem of exactly in what degree witchcraft was to be judged as heresy. Trials took
place in which both the helpless and the nobility were
accused of demonic relationships. The Bishop of
Troyes was accused of having slain by sorcery Queen
Jeanne de Navarre; the Chamberlain of France was
hanged in 1315 for having gained the Royal favour by
witchcraft; the Bishop of Cahors was executed for
having attempted to kill Pope John XXII with poison
obtained from witches.

Possibly the most interesting case history of this
period is that of Lady Alice Kyteler who was charged
with heretical sorcery in 1324. Lea in his *Materials
towards a History of Witchcraft* felt that the trial
marked 'a transition state of belief between the earlier
magic and the later witchcraft'. Certainly it was one
of the first trials in which torture was used unremit-
tingly to extract a confession.

Lady Alice was charged by her husband, Sir John le Poer, with attempts on his life by witchcraft. Her three previous husbands had died under rather obscure circumstances and the considerable wealth amassed had been passed on to the son of her first marriage, William Outlaw.

The trial was instigated by the Bishop of Ossary, Richard de Ledrede. Lady Alice, William Outlaw and their accomplices were accused of denying God, of sacrificing nine red cocks 'in the high waie' to a devil named Robert Artisson, 'one of the poorer classes of hell', of seeking knowledge of the future from devils, of making magic powders to destroy the husbands in question, of sexual intercourse with the aforementioned Robert Artisson. Witnesses claimed that they had seen Lady Alice raking the dust of the streets at twilight towards the house of William Outlaw, saying:

To the house of William, my son,
Hie all the wealth of Kilkenny town.

It was also deposed that, 'in rifling the closet of the lady, they found a Pipe of ointment, wherewith she greased a staff, upon the which she ambled and galloped through thick and thin, when and in what manner she listed' (Holinshed).

A feud ensued between Lady Alice and the Bishop. He excommunicated her, she imprisoned him. At length he succeeded in bringing the case to court, but by this time Lady Alice had fled to England. The Bishop assuaged his wrath on the members of her household. They were whipped and branded and Lady

Alice's maid, Petronilla de Meath, was put to the torture. During six bouts of flogging she confessed to all the charges. She was burned at Kilkenny in November. William Outlaw was imprisoned for nine weeks, but on his release he succeeded in having the Bishop of Ossory jailed yet again, and this time for three months.

Margaret Murray sees the trial as one of the first instances of the old and new religions coming to grips with one another; to Christina Hole it suggests the existence of a number of linked covens around Kilkenny. It is interesting to note that Lady Alice made no attempt to deny the charges brought against her. She relied on her rank as a noblewoman to save her and had little difficulty in stifling and evading the Bishop of Ossory who was, after all, an intruding Englishman attempting to put on trial a member of the old aristocracy of Ireland.

In 1398 the University of Paris took a great step forward in the definition of a pact with the devil. All superstitious observances of which the result could not reasonably be expected from God or from nature were said to constitute an implied pact. It was presumably on the basis of this conjecture that in 1474 a cock who had been sufficiently ill-advised as to lay an egg was tried, and publicly bound in Basel.

Nothing in the whole history of witchcraft, however, proved so effective as the Bull of Innocent VIII and its ensuing brainchild, the notorious *Malleus Maleficarum* variously defined as 'that very great and very wise book' by Montague Summers, and by Michelet as 'a pocket manuel of folly'. Innocent's Bull seems to have been solicited by two German Inquisitors – Kramer and Sprenger. It spoke of the terrible inroads made by witches on Northern Germany who 'by their incantations, spells, conjurations, and other accursed crimes and crafts, enormities, and horrid offences, have slain infants yet in the mother's womb, as also the offspring of cattle, have blasted the produce of the earth, the grapes of the vine, the fruits of trees, nay, men and women, beasts of burthen, herd beasts, as well as animals of other kinds . . . they hinder men from performing the sexual act and women from conceiving, whence husbands cannot know their wives nor wives receive their husbands. . . .'

The Bull enjoins 'Our Dear Sons' Kramer and Sprenger 'to be empowered without let or hindrance to proceed to the just correction, imprisonment and punishment of any persons. . . .'

The *Malleus Maleficarum* itself – the 'Hammer of Witches' – is the witch-hunter's Bible, the work which more than any other determined and directed the witch craze of the centuries that followed. It guided the minds of those judges who decided the fate of the Lancashire Witches and that of the Witches of Salem. Its opening proposition places the work in an unassailable position: 'Whether the belief that there are such beings as witches is so essential a part of the Catholic faith that obstinately to maintain the contrary opinion manifestly savours of heresy.'

From this happy starting point it defines the whole territory and operation of witchcraft and then details the means of acting against it. In its exploration of the terrain it is gullible and at times even fanciful.

For a certain man tells that, when he had lost his member, he approached a known witch to ask her to restore it to him. She told the afflicted man to climb a certain tree, and that he might take which he liked out of a nest in which there were several members. And when he tried to take a big one the witch said: You must not take that one, adding, because it belonged to a parish priest.

Malleus, Pt. 2, Qn. 1, ch. 7

There is nothing gullible or fanciful in the Inquisitors' instructions on Question 14 in Part 3 – as to whether a witch may be promised her life: 'She may be promised her life ... provided that she supply evidence which will lead to the conviction of other witches...' Her sentence is in fact life imprisonment on bread and water but 'She should be led to suppose that some other penance such as exile, will be imposed on her as punishment.' This is clemency in comparison with the other devious ways out of the dilemma:

Others think that, after she has been consigned to prison in this way, the promise to spare her life should be kept for a time, but that after a certain period she should be burned. A third opinion is that the Judge may safely promise the accused her life, but in such a way that he should afterwards disclaim the duty of passing sentence on her, deputing another judge in his place.

'Our dear sons' are equally explicit on the use of torture:

And while she is being questioned about each several point, let her be often and frequently be exposed to torture. . . . If after being fittingly tortured she refuses to tell the truth, the Judge should have other engines of torture brought before her, and tell her that she will have to endure these if she does not confess. If then she is not induced by terror to confess, the torture must be continued on the second or third day, but not repeated at that present time unless there should be some fresh indication of its probable success.

The chilling phrases are 'if she refuses to tell the truth' and 'indication of its probable success'. These are terrible warnings of the centuries of torture to follow. The only release from torture lies in confession; confession can only result in burning; obstinacy in fresh and more ingenious torture, a vicious circle from which there is no possible escape.

The ideology, the whole framework within which the systematised persecution of witches could take place, was now firmly established. As Trevor Roper puts it:

From the publication of the *Malleus* onwards, its basic content never changed. There was no further development. And yet equally there was no disintegration. It formed a reservoir of monstrous theory from which successive persecutions were fed: persecutions which did not diminish but were positively intensified in the course of the next two hundred years.

Montague Summers lists at least forty editions of the *Malleus* between 1486 and 1669. He comments: 'What is most surprising is the modernity of the book. There

is hardly a problem, a complex, a difficulty, which they have not foreseen and discussed and resolved.'
Summers' attitude is salutary to a conscience nurtured on the 19th-century liberalism of Lea or Michelet. However horrifying his attitude may be he does at least indicate the proper scale as it appeared to those at the heart of the situation from the time of Innocent VIII until the end of the 18th century. Speaking of the witches he writes: 'Had, indeed, their leaders been ready and united at the end of the seventeenth century it was planned that in practically every European country these satanic revolutionaries should rise at a given signal, when universal chaos and confusion would have reigned.'

The horror of witchcraft spread with rapidity and intensity throughout western Europe with a force and a casualty rate comparable to the bubonic plague. From a minor sectarian activity or a village curiosity it grew and raged like a forest fire that seemed certain to destroy Christianity itself.

The witches are so defiant and audacious that they say openly, if only they had an eminent and renowned man for their captain, they would become so strong and so numerous that they could march against a powerful King in pitched battle and easily vanquish him with the help of their art and their strategies.

Men became obsessed by the enormous strength of the millions of demons arrayed against them and the witches who, they were assured, were their minions:

'There are witches by the thousands everywhere mul-
tiplying upon the earth like worms in a garden.'
In the course of the two centuries that followed
witches were tortured, burned, hanged, and drowned
by thousands. It is impossible to give a wholesale estimate of the total death-toll of the witch craze. One can
only quote individual instances which give some idea
of the scale of the hysteria: 386 witches burned at
Treves in four years, 5,000 witches burned in Stras-
burg over a period of twenty years, 900 in Würzburg over eight years. The grand total for Scotland
seems to be in the region of 4,400. In Bearn De Lancue
claimed that 30,000 Basques were infected by witchcraft and burned 400 of them. Between 1486 and the
late 1660s, when the craze began at last to die down,
there can scarcely have been a week when somewhere
in Europe a witch did not burn. Whole villages were
wiped out. No one was safe, whatever their rank or
position in society. A letter from a priest named Duren
who lived in a village near Bonn in the early 17th
century gives some idea of what daily life was like at
the height of the persecutions.

Half the city must be implicated, for already professors,
law students, pastors, canons, vicars and monks have been
arrested and burned. . . . The Chancellor and his wife and
the Private Secretary's wife have already been appre-
hended and executed. On the Eve of Our Lady's Day there
was executed here a girl of nineteen who had the reputation of being the loveliest and most virtuous in all the city
and who from her childhood had been brought up by the
Prince Bishop himself. A canon of the cathedral named

Rotensahe, I saw beheaded and burned. Children of three or four years have devils for their paramours. Students and boys of noble birth, of nine, ten, eleven, twelve, thirteen and fourteen years of age, have been burned. To sum up, things are in such a pitiful state that one does not know with what people one may talk and associate.

Witchcraft was regarded as an offence so terrible that no punishment could be too severe. 'Whatever punishment we can order against witches by roasting and cooking them over a slow fire is not really very much,' wrote Jean Bodin. Nothing that man could devise would be as bad as 'the eternal agonies which are prepared for them in hell, for the fire here cannot last much more than an hour or so until the witches have died'.

Confession was widely regarded as an essential element in the course of bringing a witch to justice and to this end torture was freely applied. Hartwig von Dassel, writing in 1597, states that great labour must be required in the torturing of witches since that by the aid of the devil they are rendered so insensible that they would suffer themselves to be torn limb from limb rather than confess. Wilhelm Pressel gives us a full account of the first day's torture of a woman accused of witchcraft in Prossneck in 1629.

The proceedings start early in the morning. The woman's hands are bound, the hangman cuts her hair and throws alcohol over her head, setting it on fire to burn it to its roots. He then places strips of sulphur in her armpits and burns them. She is hauled up to the ceiling and left hanging there for three hours while the hangman enjoys a leisurely breakfast. Thus refreshed he throws alcohol over her back and burns it, suspends her from the ceiling with heavy weights on her feet, forces her body down on a plank stuck with nails, squeezes her thumbs and big toes in a vice, and hangs her from the ceiling again. During this period she faints several times.

He then squeezes her legs in a vice and follows this with flogging with a rawhide whip. He puts her thumbs and big toes back into the vice and goes out to lunch for three hours. The afternoon consists largely of whipping.

It is small wonder that the accused confessed:

Her feet were crushed and her body stretched out to greater length, she screamed piteously and said all was true that they had demanded of her: she drank the blood of children whom she stole on her night flights and she had murdered about sixty infants. She named twenty other women who had been with her at the sabbats, and said the wife of a late burgomaster presided over the fights and banquets.

Johannes Junius, a Burgomaster of Bamberg accused of witchcraft in 1628, wrote to his daughter:

When at last the executioner led me back into the cell he said to me, 'Sir, I beg you, for God's sake, confess something whether it be true or not. Invent something, for you cannot endure the torture which you will be put to: and even if you bear it all, yet you will not escape, not even if you were an earl, but one torture will follow another until you say you are a witch.'

1. & 2. Two witches, both wearing the pointed hats generally associated with their trade. *Above*. Jane Caudwell. *Below*. Jane Scrimshaw.

3. The devil or 'the black goat' and the witches lighting
their candles. From *Compendium Maleficarum* by Guazzo.

4. Early print of the trial of a witch at Salem.

5. Mrs. Eleanor Bone, High Priestess of two covens, one in Tooting Bec and one in Cumberland.

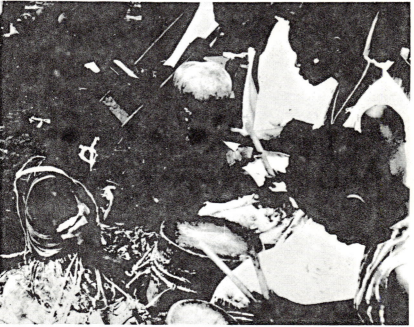

6. *Above.* This picture of a witchdoctor's ceremony in Azande shows the magic implements arranged in a circle.
7. *Below.* Kenyan witchdoctor casting out spirits.

8. Gerald Gardner.

9. Aleister Crowley, 'The Great Beast'.

10. Mia Farrow as Rosemary, when she sees her 'baby'. The witchcraft theme of *Rosemary's Baby* was tragically echoed when Sharon Tate, wife of the director, Roman Polanski, was murdered, allegedly by a sect calling themselves the 'Cult of Satan'.

He made his confession – he had renounced God, had been baptised by the devil, had a succubus called Vixen, rode to the sabbat on a black dog etc. He wrote: 'It is all sheer lies and inventions, so help me God. If God sends no means of bringing the truth to light, our whole kindred will be burned. God in heaven knows that I know not the slightest thing. I die innocent and as a martyr.' He was burned some six weeks after he was first brought to trial.

In many cases the questions were standardised. A woman would be asked when had she received the devil's marks or what was the name of her incubus or what the ointment she rubbed on her broomstick was made of, and she would be tortured until a satisfactory answer was obtained.

Inasmuch as her answers are unsatisfactory and she still seems under the domination of the devil, she is tied with ropes in order to receive a flogging. Several lashes are administered. Thereupon she confesses that fifteen years ago, she buried in the garden the powder she had received from the devil, in the hope that it would cause bad weather and prevent the fruit from ripening that year.

Eichstaff trial, 1637

In England torture was not practised. To some extent this accounts for the low figure of executions (witches were hanged and not burned) in comparison with France and Germany. Suspected witches were stripped and examined for the devil's marks, they were pricked with long pins for insensitive areas of flesh (also the work of the devil), they were deprived of sleep, they were swum. There was, however, no need to obtain a full confession. Witches were convicted on the depositions of witnesses.

England was free, too, from the highly organised persecutions of the Inquisition and by and large suffered nothing comparable to the witch hunts organised by such enthusiasts as the Prince Bishops of Würzburg and Bamberg. The great exception to all this was the self-styled Witch Finder General, Matthew Hopkins. Under the reign of Charles I, the persecution of witches had all but died out in England, but with the breakdown of law and order that accompanied the Civil War it was possible for a man like Hopkins to impose himself virtually unimpeded on the bewildered townships of East Anglia. The general public needed no encouragement to see witches everywhere:

In good sooth, I may tell it to you as to my friend, when I go but into my closet I am afraid, for I see now and then a hare; which my conscience giveth me is a witch, or some witches' spirit she so stareth at me.

Gifford; A Dialogue concerning witches
and witchcraft, 1603

Hopkins did not have to go far to find his first witches:

He had some seven or eight of that horrible sect of witches living in the town where he lived, a town in Essex called Manningtree, with diverse and adjacent witches of other towns, who every six weeks in the night (being always on the Friday night) had their meeting close to his house, and had their several solemn sacrifices there offered to the devil.

His first deposition was against Elizabeth Clarke, an old woman with one leg. In this he was aided by his assistants John Stearne and Mary Phillipps. Elizabeth Clarke confessed to carnal copulation with the devil and Hopkins swore on oath that he and Stearne had seen within a quarter of an hour four imps go to Elizabeth Clarke in the shapes of a white dog, a greyhound, a polecat, and a black imp. The woman was hanged.

Witch mania spread like a fever across East Anglia. Twenty-five were hanged in Chelmsford, sixty in Bury St Edmunds. Hopkins' reputation grew steadily and he became a rich man. Between them, he and Stearne must have earned themselves at least a thousand pounds.

Although Hopkins was not empowered to use torture he came as near to it as he was able. 'Swimming' was a technique he employed a good deal in the first months of his campaign but the parliamentary commission of oyer and terminer of 1645 came down heavily against this form of investigation – 'an abominable, inhumane and unmerciful trial of these poor creatures'. However, Hopkins' combination of 'walking' and 'watching' generally proved sufficiently effective. John Lowes, a parson seventy years old, was broken by Hopkins' assistants who 'kept him awake several nights together, and ran him backwards and forwards about the room until he was out of breath.

Then they rested him a little and then ran him again. And thus they did for several days and nights together, till he was weary of his life and was scarcely sensible of what he said or did.' He confessed that he had caused a ship to sink off Harwich in calm weather and that he had bewitched cattle. He recited his own burial service on his way to the scaffold.

Eventually Hopkins' power began to wane. A magazine called *The Moderate Intelligencer* commented 'Life is precious and there is need of great inquisition before it is taken away.' A clergyman preached against him, although he rapidly recanted on Hopkins' approach. Hopkins was sensible enough to see that it was time to retire. He died in his bed in Bury St Edmunds. There is no certain record of how many he had caused to be hanged. 400 would seem to be a reasonably conservative estimate. The question inevitably arises, did everyone accept unquestioningly the wholesale persecutions? What had the philosophers and the men of law to say about it?

Montaigne approached the matter with his usual ironic scepticism: 'I saw both proofs, witnesses, voluntary confessions and some other insensible marks about this miserable old woman. I enquired and talked with her a long time, with the greatest heed at caution I could, yet am I not easily carried away by preoccupation. In the end and in my conscience, I should rather have appointed them helleborum than hemlock.' He concludes: 'When all is done it is an overvaluing of one's conjectures by them to cause a man to be burned alive.'

Hobbes characteristically dismisses the whole issue with some vigour: 'The enemy has been here in the night of our natural ignorance and sown the tares of Spiritual errors.' He denounces the 'demonology of the Heathen poets, that is to say, their fabulous doctrine concerning Demons, which are but idols and phantasms of the brain.'

Bacon is rational but cautious: 'For the witches themselves are imaginative and believe oft-times they do that which they do not: and people are credulous in that point and ready to impute accidents and natural operations to witchcraft.'

Ralegh is even more cautious:

These men are distract, as they believe that by terrible words they make the devil to tremble; that being once impaled in a circle (a circle which cannot keep out a mouse) they therein, as they suppose and ensconce themselves against the great monster . . . whereas in very truth, the obedience which devils seem to use, is but thereby to possess themselves of the bodies and souls of those which raise them up; as his Majesty in his book hath excellently taught.

History of the World

In fairness to Ralegh it must be pointed out that he was himself in a vulnerable position through his association with the 'School of Night' and his words may merely be a form of self-protection against James.

There is, however, a curious reluctance to speak out. The problem is considered intellectually and philosophically, but rarely are the activities of the witch persecutors denounced. Reginald Scot's *Discovery of Witchcraft* is remarkable in this respect. He does not deny the possible existence of witchcraft but firmly speaks out against the prevalence of superstition and persecution: 'Such faithless people (I say) are also persuaded, that neither hail nor snow, thunder nor lightning, rain nor tempestuous winds come from the heavens at the commandment of God: but are raised by the cunning power of witches and conjurers: insomuch as a clap of thunder or a gale of wind is no sooner heard, but either they run – to ring bells or cry out to burn witches.' His book was burned by the command of James I.

The trials themselves seem to have run their course without opposition or hindrance. A witch might strangle herself in her cell to avoid further torture, but the persecutions seem to have taken place among almost total public acquiescence. Ralph Gardiner in *England's Grievance Discovered in Relation to the Coal Trade* gives an instance of interference in a witch hunt that is almost unique. The Borough of Newcastle on Tyne in 1649 was employing a celebrated Scottish witch-pricker to seek out witches. Some thirty women had been stripped, pricked, and judged guilty. A personable and good looking woman was accused and the witch-pricker went about his task:

Presently in sight of all the people, he laid her body naked to the waist, with all her clothes over her head by which fright and shame, all her blood contracted into one part of her body, and then he ran a pin into her thigh, and then suddenly let her coats fall, and then demanded she had nothing of him in her body but did not bleed, but she being much amazed replied little, and then he put his hand up her coats and pulled out the pin and set aside as a guilty person and child of the Devil.

At this point a certain Colonel Hobhouse intervened. He insisted that the woman be called again and ordered the Scot to stick the pin in again in the same spot. He did so, the blood flowed and the woman cried out. She was cleared of suspicion and the witch-pricker who was paid twenty shillings a conviction was somewhat discomfited.

The fear of witchcraft died slowly. In England the last trial took place in 1712 and the accused, Jane Wenham, although convicted by an hysterical jury, was freed by a Royal Pardon. In Germany in 1749 Marie Renata, the sub-prioress of a Convent near Wurzburg, was put to the torture and burned during one of those periodic fits of hysteria that seemed to sweep nunneries at regular intervals in the 17th and 18th centuries. Her confession was much the same as those two hundred years earlier: she had pierced the host with nails at the Sabbat, she had copulated with the Devil, she had three cats who were her familiars. In France, witchcraft lingered on well into the age of reason. A man was executed for ligature in Bordeaux in 1718, a priest was burned for Divination in Lyons in 1745. In Seville in 1818 Ana Barbero was sentenced to 200 lashes for making a pact with the Devil.

In 1692 there was an extraordinary outbreak of witchcraft fever in New England. John Evelyn recorded in his diary in London: 'Unheard of stories

of the universal increase of witches in New England;
men, women and children devoting themselves to the
Devil, so as to threaten the subversion of the govern-
ment.' The unhappy record of the trials at Salem
demonstrates on the one hand how firm and unchanged
through centuries was the tradition of witchcraft belief
and yet reveals almost for the first time man obsessed
with doubt and self-questioning about the validity of
what they were at. The small puritan communities of
Massachusetts who had fought off Indians on the war-
path, small-pox, and freezing cold, suddenly found
itself in the front line in man's constant battle with
the powers of Darkness:

The New-Englanders are a people of God settled in those,
which were once the Devil's territories; and it may easily
be supposed that the Devil was exceedingly disturbed,
when he perceived such a people here accomplishing the
promise of old made unto our Blessed Jesus that he should
have the utmost parts of the earth for his possession ... the
Devil thus irritated, immediately tried all sorts of methods
to overturn this poor plantation. . . . I believe that never
were more Satanical devices used for the unsettling of any
people under the sun than what have been employed for
the extirpation of the Vine which God has here planted.
        Cotton Mather, *Wonders of the Invisible World*

It is this conviction that the whole state was in
danger that gives the Salem trials their particular
character. Hale spoke of 'the design to destroy Salem
village and to begin at the Minister's house, and to
destroy the Church of God and to set up Satan's King-
dom'. Cotton Mather had heard that 'At prodigious

witch meetings the wretches have proceeded so far as to concert and consult the methods of rooting out the Christian religion from this country and setting up instead of it, perhaps a more gross diabolism than ever the world saw before.'

Amid scenes of extraordinary hysteria, made familiar now to us by Arthur Miller's *The Crucible*, more than one hundred and forty persons were accused and at least twenty-three were hanged, pressed to death, or died in jail. Five were reprieved, two pleaded pregnancy and one, Mary Bradbury, escaped.

As Chadwick Hansen has demonstrated in his recent study of the trials something was definitely going on at Salem. Bridget Bishop, Candy and Wilmot Redd had been experimenting with black magic, and Dorcas Hoar had carried her palmistry into the field of divination. The Reverend George Burroughs, who may have practised witchcraft, had boasted of extraordinary powers:

He was a very puny man yet he had often done things beyond the strength of a giant. A gun of about seven foot barrel, and so heavy that strong men could not steadily hold it out with hands; there were several testimonies given in by persons of Credit and Honour that he made nothing of taking up such a gun behind the lock, with but one hand and holding it out like a Pistol at Arms-End. G. B. in his Vindication was so foolish as to say that an Indian was there and held it out at the same time: whereas none of the spectators even saw such Indian; but they supposed the Black Man (as the witches call the devil, and they generally say he resembles an Indian) might give him that assistance.

It must always be remembered that the inhabitants of Salem were in an entrenched situation. They were strangers 'in a corner of the world where the Devil had reigned without any control for many eyes'. The Indians were a constant threat and traffic with them becomes inextricably confused with the witchcraft evidence: 'There stands Alden! He sells powder and shot to the Indians and French, and lies with Indian squaws and has Indian papooses.'

Yet when confessions are obtained, they are the confessions of Chelmsford or Northampton or Faversham:

She and Martha Carrier did both ride on a stick or pole when they went to the witch meeting at Salem village, and that the stick broke as they were carried in the air over the tops of the trees, and they fell. But she did hang fast about the neck of Goody Carrier and were presently at the village, that she was then much hurt of her leg.

The trials did not take place without a great deal of doubt and self questioning. Torture, which even Cotton Mather had condemned as 'un-English' was employed, but its use was hotly debated. John Proctor, who was later to be hanged as a witch, protested firmly against the means by which the evidence implicating him had been obtained: 'Two of the five are young men who would not confess anything till they tied them neck and heads till the blood was ready to come out of their noses. . . . These actions are very like the Popish cruelties.'

There was much brooding over the nature of the 'spectral' evidence, the hysterical ravings of the little gang of girls that they were afflicted and tortured by various members of the community. Cotton Mather wrote: 'I do think that when there is no further evidence against a person but only this, that a specter in their shape does afflict a neighbour, that evidence is not enough to convict of witchcraft.' Nevertheless he allowed that 'a very great use is to be made of the spectral impressions upon the sufferers. They justly introduce and determine an inquiry into the circumstances of the person accused, and they strengthen other presumptions.'

It was by such equivocal thinking that John Proctor was hanged. Cotton's father, Increase, brooded at length on the problem of:

Whether it is not possible for the Devil to impose on the imagination of persons bewitched, and to cause them to believe that an Innocent, yea that a Pious person does torment them, when the Devil himself doth it; or whether Satan may not appear in the Shape of an Innocent and Pious, as well as of a Nocent and wicked person, to afflict such as suffer by Diabolical Molestations.

But he promptly evaded the issue, convinced, as were so many commentators on witchcraft, that the Devil could only operate within the permission of God.

It has very seldom been known that Satan has personated innocent men doing an ill thing, but Providence has found out some way for their Vindication; either they have been able to prove that they were in another place when Fact was done, or the like. So that perhaps there never was an Instance of any innocent person condemned in any Court of Judicature on Earth, only through Satan's deluding and imposing on the Imaginations of Man, when nevertheless, the Witnesses, Juries and Judges were all to be excused from blame.

One can only marvel at Mather's bland optimism, particularly in view of what followed:

We confess that we ourselves were not capable to understand, nor able to withstand the mysterious delusions of the Powers of Darkness and Prince of the Air; but were, for want of knowledge in ourselves and better information from others, prevailed with to take up such evidence against the accused, as on further consideration and better information, we justly fear was unsufficient for touching the lives of any.

Confession of Error by the Jurors of Salem, 1692

'Insufficient' for twenty-three lives at the wholesale destruction of the life of a community.

The emphasis placed on the religion of Satan throughout the centuries of witch persecution makes it virtually impossible to trace exactly what was going on. So much is laid down as the testimony of witnesses, so much is confessed that one cannot see the wood for the trees. It is clearly impossible to accept, as did Montague Summers and Margaret Murray, all that was confessed as absolute truth. Yet it is equally impossible to deny that anything was happening at all. Lucy Mair in her study of witchcraft has written:

What has been obscured by the famous trials, either of

heretics or of persons accused of conspiring against princes, is the possibility that to less exalted people the belief in witchcraft was very much what it is in Africa, an explanation of misfortune in terms of the ill-will of neighbours, and that most of the trials of witches were concerned with situations of this kind.

On the village level – spells, philtres, charms – witchcraft certainly existed in the manner in which it always existed and always will. But the religion of the witches is largely a question of organisation and the central problem of any historical approach to witchcraft is to determine whether witchcraft was a sporadic and an individual activity or an organised and directed one.

Montague Summers, in his introduction to the *Demonolatry* of Nicholas Remy, states categorically that 'at the end of the sixteenth century France was literally honeycombed by the vast secret society of witches, whose members, ever busy at their evil work, might be found everywhere, in crowded capital and remote hamlet, in palace and cottage, of both sexes and all ages, even the very youngest.' This was certainly how many men at the time regarded the situation and it is worth considering the means by which witchcraft could form the basis of an organised secret society. Kittredge asserted that 'There is not the slightest evidence that witches were ever organised at all', but Margaret Murray detected, or believed she detected, the basic unit of witchcraft activity in the form of the coven.

Margaret Murray's theory assumes that the confessions of the witches embodies the truth. The confession that is central to her argument is that of Isobel Gowdie, a Scottish witch from Auldearne who in 1662 made four wholly voluntary confessions. Isobel Gowdie claimed that she had been initiated by the highest authority:

As I was going between the farmsteads of Drumdewin and the Heads, I met the Devil, and there covenanted in a manner with him, and I promised to meet him in the night time in the Kirk of Auldearne, which I did. And the first thing I did on that night was to deny my baptism, and did put on hand on the crown of my head and the other to the sole of my foot and then gave all between my two hands to the devil.

Much of her confession is fantasy stemming from a highly responsive and powerful imagination:

We fly like straws when we please; wild-straws and corn-stalks serve as horses for us, and we put them between our legs and say: 'Horse and hatlock in the Devil's name!' And if anyone sees these straws in a whirlwind and does not bless himself, we may shoot him dead at our pleasure.

But her statements about the organisation of the coven and the daily organisation of witchcraft have a disturbing feeling of authenticity about them. 'The last time that our Coven met we and another Coven were dancing at the Hill of Earlseat ... and the other Coven being at Downiehills we went beside them ...' She describes how they fashioned an image of clay to destroy 'the Earl of Park's healthy children'. 'Only we were at the making of it, but all the multitude of our

Covens got notice of it at the next meeting ... all my own Coven got notice of it very shortly.'

She also stated that 'Jean Mairten is Maiden to our Coven. John Young is officer to our Coven. There are thirteen persons in every coven.' The coven officer seems to have fulfilled the office of the devil. The coven met weekly to exchange of information, to determine what actions were to be carried out by them as a group, to allot punishments and disciplines where necessary, to feast and to dance.

Apart from the feasting and dancing it must have all been rather like a board meeting. Everything that was discussed was entered in a register. Attendance seems to have been compulsory. Margaret Murray found eighteen examples of such covens, although she had to bend facts and figures a little to do so, and there does seem evidence enough to suggest some kind of communal activity afoot in Pendle Forest, in Maidstone, in Faversham, and even in Salem.

The celebrated trials at North Berwick (1590–92), in which James I took a participating interest, reveal – in so far as evidence produced by torture can reveal anything – a mammoth corporate activity involving some 200 witches. They put to sea each with a riddle or sieve to sink, presumably by sympathetic magic, the King's ship on its passage to Denmark. 'Also, on his majesty's return, Satan raised a mist, by throwing something like a football in the sea, and this was done that James might be cast upon the English shore.' James held 'that they were all extreme liars' but Agnes Sampson, the eldest and most impressive of the witches, took the

King on one side and 'declared unto him the very words which passed between the King's Majesty and his Queen at Upslo in Norway, the first night of their marriage'. The King was seriously alarmed 'and swore by the living God, that he believed that all the Devils in hell could not have discovered the same'.

From the activities of the coven, we must pass to the larger and even more conjectural organisation of the Sabbat. The festival of the witches was said to be celebrated on February 2 (Candlemas), Walpurgis night (April 30), St John's Eve (June 23), Lammas Day (August 1), All Hallows Eve (October 31), St Thomas' Eve (December 21); although there are suggestions that Sabbats were in fact held every week in conjunction with the coven meeting. The numbers of witches taking part is reported as varying from one hundred to ten thousand. De Lancre wrote: 'The Sabbat resembles a fair of merchants, mingling together, angry and half crazed, arriving from all quarters, a surging crowd of some hundred thousand devotees of Satan.'

What is alleged to have taken place at the Sabbat is best left to the commentators on witchcraft and to the confessions of the witches themselves.

Before they go to the Sabbat they anoint themselves upon some part of their bodies with an unguent made from various foul and filthy ingredients ... so anointed they are carried away on a cowl staff or broom, or a reed, or a cleft stick, or a distaff, which things they ride.

He set us upon a beast and carried us over churches and high walls.

They were suddenly carried through the air to a place where they found four women and six devils in the form of men, but very ugly to look upon.

There in the synagogue common to other witches, sorcerers, heretical enchanters and worshippers of demons, by the light of a noisesome fire, after many jubilations, dancings, feastings, drinkings and games in honour of the presiding Beelzebub, Prince of Demons, in the form and appearance of a most black and filthy goat, you have adored him as God, by acts and words, approaching him suppliantly on your knees, offering him lighted candles of pitch, kissing with the utmost reverence and a sacriligious mouth his most nasty and stinking anus.

The devil made us kiss his mouth, then his navel, then his virile member, then his arse.

She affirmed that she had often seen the devil couple with a multitude of women who she knew by name and surname, and that it was the devil's custom to have intercourse with the beautiful women from the front and with the ugly from the rear.

She said she feared intercourse with the devil because his member was scaly and caused extreme pain; furthermore his semen was extremely cold, so cold that she had never become pregnant by him.

Alexia Drigie examined her devil's penis when it was sticking up and said it was always so long as some kitchen utensils, which then happened to be in view.

There was found in the place where they danced a round circle wherein there was the manifest marks of the treading of cloven feet which were seen from the day they were

first discovered till the next winter that the plough cast
them out.

Such is the nature of the Sabbat. There is unhappily
very little evidence that is not the work of a crazed
fanatic witch-hunter or the result of a confession extracted after prolonged torture. It is possible to see
behind all this a festivity in which the witches anointed
and drugged themselves, danced, drank, feasted indulged in indiscriminate intercourse, worshipped a
man impersonating the devil, and were penetrated by
him with an artificial penis made of stone or iron.

We must remember, though, that the accusations
levelled against the witches are exactly the same as
those used to denounce the Cathari several centuries
earlier. Their meetings were known as the Synagogue
Satanue. They too anointed themselves and 'flew
through the air' to meetings, they too were accused of
child sacrifice. The Waldensians were also accused
of meeting by night to worship the devil with orgiastic
rituals, as were Stedlingers, Luciferans, and even the
Knights Templar. On the one hand this may be evidence of continuing ritual, but it is much more likely
that the church had found a convenient stick with
which to beat its enemies. On the eve of the witch craze
in 1375, when the Cathars and the Waldensians had
been crushed, an inquisitor, Nicholas Eneric, com-
plained about his lack of employment: 'At the present
time there are no rich heretics, and in consequence
princes, not seeing the prospect of obtaining much
money, will not commit themselves to any great ex-

penditure. It is a shame that so beneficial an institution as ours should find its future so uncertain.'

The sheer quantity of the evidence – the voluntary and enforced confessions, the pamphlets and encyclicals, the learned discourses – should not be allowed to overwhelm the judgment when looking at the witch persecutions. One should remember the investigation carried out by a member of the Inquisition in Spain, Alonso de Salazar Frias, in 1611. Over a period of eight months he talked to 1,800 witches, many of whom had made voluntary confessions, and sifted through a vast amount of testimony. He concluded:

Considering the above with all the Christian attention in my power, I have not found even indications from which to infer that a single act of witchcraft has really occurred. . . . I also feel certain that, under present conditions, there is no need of fresh edicts or the prolongation of those existing but rather that, in the diseased state of the public mind, every agitation of the matter is harmful and increases the evil. I deduce the importance of silence, and reserve from the experience that these were neither witches nor bewitched until they were talked and written about.

6

Modern Satanists

How art thou fallen from Heaven, O Lucifer, son of the
morning! (Isaiah, xiv, 12)
I beheld Satan as lightning fall from Heaven
(St Luke, x, 18)

As we have seen, modern witches in Europe and
America believe that they are the inheritors of a religion more ancient than Christianity. Logically, therefore, their rituals can have little in common with either
the Christian or the Jewish faith as both the Old and
the New Testaments were preached to the pagans of
Europe at roughly the same time. So that, if these
modern witches are sincere, the charge of worshipping
the Judeo-Christian Satan cannot be laid at their door.
In fact, modern 'Satanists' and 'Luciferians', whose
cults are fairly evenly spread throughout Britain,
France, Germany, and the United States, are united in
their patronising, rather contemptuous attitude to the
'Gardnerian' type of witch.

Although both witches and 'Satanists' share the
beliefs that magic can be used to achieve actual physi-

cal results, witches reject all Biblical teaching out of
hand, while the Satanists, through the very nature of
their beliefs, accept both God – 'Yahwe' – and Satan,
as with other superhuman beings.
The term Satanist, curiously enough, was first used
to denote those who believed in nothing at all. John
Aylmer, Bishop of London under Queen Elizabeth I,
described the atheists of his day as Satanists in his
pamphlet *An Harbour for Faithful and True Subjects*
published in 1559. 'Satanists' of the modern type –
literally worshippers of Satan – appear to have come
into being in France some two hundred years before
Aylmer wrote his pamphlet, when the first 'black
masses' were celebrated. These were parodies of the
Christian mass. Some, such as the 'Mass of St Secaire'
which was practised in Gascony and Brittany, actually
had this efficacy of the Catholic mass – although it
was a requiem mass said for the living. By this means
it was believed that the person named during the celebration of the ritual could be brought to an untimely
death. Other forms of 'mass' used a toad or piece of
turnip instead of the Host, and a filthy mixture of
blood, urine, and feces in place of the sacramental
wine. For sociological and political reasons these early
forms of the black mass were popular throughout the
Middle Ages. In many cases a hated political figure
would be represented by the toad which, after being
baptised in his name, was sacrificed painfully by the
officiant – thus wishing the same fate on the enemy,
and at the same time allowing some vicarious relief to
the feelings of the oppressed congregation.

The notorious Madame Le Voisin, executed in Paris in February 1680, was one of the innovators of the modern black mass, in that the forms her ritual took are largely used today. La Voisin exceeded most of her modern imitators, however, using babies as sacrificial offerings to her Satanic master – although her practice of blackmailing the many high officials who were unfortunate enough to be drawn into her circle is a danger to be faced by any person inadvisedly joining a modern Satanist group. La Voisin's most celebrated follower was Madame de Montespan, mistress of Louis XIV, who offered her naked body as a 'living altar' in order that she might retain the love of her royal master.

The 18th century probably marked the peak of Satanism, when rich young 'bucks' in every capital of Europe indulged in orgies of sacrifice to Satan, perverted sexual activities, and gluttonous hedonism of all kinds. La Voisin's impieties had found followers in Germany, Italy, and Britain, and in the first twenty years of the 18th century bodies of young aristocrats banded themselves together for the purpose of blasphemy and total sensual excess. The 'Hell Fire Clubs', as they were called, knew no frontiers and certainly no limitations. In 1721 King George I, appalled at the lengths to which his young courtiers were going, issued an order in Council to curb these 'horrible impieties'.

The *Gazette*, on April 29, 1721, commented: 'The members of these clubs meet and in the most impious and blasphemous manner insult the most sacred Principles of our Holy Religion and affront Almighty God Himself.' The King was resolved, went on the report,

to 'make use of all the Authority committed to him by
Almighty God, to punish such enormous Offenders,
and to crush such shocking impieties before they increase and draw down the Vengeance of God upon this
nation'.

It was discovered that the principal Hell Fire Club
in Britain had various headquarters; at Somerset
House in the Strand, in Westminster, and in a house
in Conduit Street near Hanover Square. The Presi-
dent of the club was named 'King of Hell' and before
long it became common knowledge that the 'King of
Hell' in this case was Philip, Lord Wharton.

The most famous of all British Hell Fire Clubs was
that which met at Medmenham Abbey on the banks of
the River Thames and went under the title of the
'Medmenham Monks'.

No one knows exactly the date of the foundation of
this unholy 'order' but the figure most closely tied in
with it was Sir Francis Dashwood, Baron Le Despencer,
Chancellor of the Exchequer and landowner at West
Wycombe, Buckinghamshire. Dashwood had a propen-
sity for dressing in monk's habit; the painter Knapton
depicted him in 1742 dressed in monkish attire adoring
a naked figure of Venus. Ten years later the Medmenham Monks were in full swing, with Sir Francis at their
head and a membership comprising many of the most
influential men of the day: John Wilkes, Montagu,
Earl of Sandwich, John Churchill, Lord Melcombe, and
George Selwyn were a few of them. Many stories are
told of the wild and perverse activities of the 'Monks'.
Defrocked priests officiated at obscene ceremonies,

women and young men were sexually assaulted, and the resulting scandal shocked every court in Europe. And yet Dashwood's best – or worst – efforts were exceeded by those of his counterparts in Ireland.

There, in the Eagle Tavern in Dublin City and at a remote hunting lodge on Montpelier Hill near Rathfarnam, Irish noblemen met for the express purpose of scandalising the poorer population and, in particular, the Roman Catholic hierarchy. Their leaders were, as in England, from the highest strata of society; young men who by virtue of birth and finance felt entitled to do what they wished. The founder of the Dublin branch of the Hell Fire Club was Richard Parsons, first Earl of Rosse, and his members included Peter Lens, a miniature painter of note who was also a professed follower of Satan, Colonel Jack St Leger – descendant of Anthony St Leger who had been three times Governor of Ireland in the 16th century, and brother of the founder of the St Leger classic race – a Mrs Blenderhasett, whose sexual excesses exhausted even the capacities of her male counterparts, and Richard Chappel Whaley, father of one of the most notorious rakes of all, Thomas 'Buck' Whaley. Richard was known as 'Burnchapel' Whaley because of his habit of riding around on Sunday mornings tossing blazing torches into the thatch of Catholic chapels on the outskirts of Dublin. His son exceeded him even in this. Like his father, Thomas was a pyromaniac and a gambler, as well as possessing the normal carnal appetites of his compatriots – those involving sex and drink. In the club he frequented – Daly's, on St Stephens Green –

it was common for any member found cheating to be thrown from the gaming room window to his messy though sudden death some thirty feet below. But Thomas Whaley managed to elude this unpleasant end on several occasions by ruse. During one riotous night he bet a fellow member of the club that he could leap from the window without coming to harm. The wager involved several thousand pounds. Whaley promptly went to his stables, selected a sound horse, brought it into the gaming room and rode it through the window panes. The horse broke several bones and had to be destroyed; Whaley broke none and won his bet. On another occasion, a £20,000 wager with a prominent Duke, he undertook to walk to Jerusalem, except where the sea intervened, play fives against the Wailing Wall, and return within twelve months. He won his bet again and, because of the gamble and because of his additional boast that he had been drunk in all the Holy Places, was known for the rest of his life as 'Jerusalem' Whaley.

His father's arsonist tendencies came out in Thomas; according to legend it was he who, during a Black Mass at Montpelier Hill, accidentally burned the house down and in the process killed several of his companions. A butler, so the story goes, spilled drink on his suit. In a fit of rage Thomas poured a bottle of brandy over the butler's head and set light to the unfortunate man. Screaming in agony, the butler fell against a tapestry, and within seconds the whole place was an inferno. Many Hell Fire Club members, too drunk to move, were killed in the blaze, though Thomas Whaley himself escaped. Another tale has it that, at a meeting in Paris, international 'hell raisers' of the period realised that the only abomination they had left untried was that of cannibalism. Whaley, ever the one for an adventure, undertook to provide the necessary carcass. He set a gin trap on his land outside Dublin, caught a pretty young local girl, killed her, had her smoked in his ham-curing barn, cut her into joints and sent these to his friends abroad.

Whaley's end was as spectacular as his life. For years he had embraced Satanism as the only religion seeking, in his own words, 'a pleasure and happiness that I never found' and dissipating a fortune of £400,000 in the process. At the age of thirty-four, while travelling from Liverpool to London, he stopped at Knutsford, Cheshire, and died in the Royal George Hotel there. The year was 1800, and the gay, abandoned days of the Irish 'Hell Fire Bucks' had gone some years before. According to local records an Irishman, one Mr Robinson, was present when Whaley's body was encoffined and, grabbing a set of bagpipes leaped onto the coffin and began to accompany his dancing in a hornpipe – an action of which, in his more rakish days, Whaley would surely have approved.

Whaley, as we have seen, died in 1800, at the dawn of the sensible, scientific, 19th century. With the coming of railways, iron-clad ships, and automatic spinning looms, the medieval concept of magic and witchcraft seemed to recede. Again the aristocracy of the day, though still comfortable in their great country houses, waited upon by innumerable servants and surrounded by dogs and horses, had not the freedom of Whaley and St Leger. The French Revolution had perhaps sounded a warning note; the peasantry were not to be lightly ill-treated in the way that they had been.

But the perverse emotions which had caused the debauches of the old Hell Fire Clubs did not die out so quickly. Satan continues to be worshipped and – as the brutal murder of American actress Sharon Tate at the hands of a 'Satanist' cult shows – his followers are still capable of viciousness and cruelty. More often than not, however, the modern Satan worshipper is after sexual thrills rather than murderous ones. Rome, according to many occultists, has long been the centre for Black Masses in Italy, while Paris also caters for Satan's brood. It is interesting that both cities possess a high proportion of Roman Catholics, and it is tempting to speculate on whether this fact adds an element of extra spice to the proceedings. According to one source, defrocked priests can be hired – for a price – to officiate at Black Masses in most big Continental cities, and the stealing of consecrated wafers for use when an ordained priest cannot be made available is easy enough in a society where a large body of people are daily communicants. The Satanist merely receives Holy Communion in the normal way and then slips the Host from his mouth and into a handkerchief.

Most people are familiar with the traditional 'horror story' setting for a Black Mass; few people who have not attended one realise the terror and the nausea which the event can produce in real life, even in 'non-involved sightseers'.

A ruined or deserted church is favoured by Satanists for their rituals, although open air Black Masses have been said in the rambling, overgrown cemeteries of Paris quite often in recent years. Usually, the venue is a large house in the suburbs, away from main roads and the prying eyes of neighbours.

The Mass begins at eleven o'clock, timed so that it shall finish on the stroke of midnight. The altar is covered with a black cloth, on which stand six black candles, a chalice, and an upturned crucifix. Sometimes a representation of Satan stands in the centre of the altar behind the crucifix. In front of the cross, spread-eagled so that her thighs hang over the edge, lies a naked woman. In either hand she holds a black candle, and it is on her bare stomach that the priest 'consecrates' the host – often dyed red or black, and triangular in shape.

Serge Kordeiv, a photographer who now lives in Kent, England, attended one such ceremony and still remembers with horror the things he witnessed there.

The atmosphere was almost unbearable, repulsive and at the same time weakening; one felt almost immediately light-headed on entering the room. The black candles seemed to contain pitch and stank abominably. Their smell was partly masked by a brazier of incense which stood to the left of the altar and which, I suspect, also contained hashish. Over these odours was the hot reek of sweating naked bodies; everyone left his or her clothes outside the room and apart from black face masks all were entirely nude.

The priest was a heavily built man with red hair; he

walked down an aisle formed by the congregation until he stood between the legs of the girl on the altar. Slipping out of the heavy cloak he was wearing, he handed it to one of the two acolytes, one a man, the other a woman, who knelt at either side of him. He kissed the girl on the altar three times – on the breasts and on the genitals – and then proceeded to say the Mass. It was exactly the same as a normal Catholic Mass except that the name of Satan had been substituted for that of Christ.

At the consecration, while bending over the chalice on the girl's stomach, the priest pulled her slightly towards him and had sexual intercourse with her.

'To my horror the girl started to scream and moan,' recalls Kordeiv, 'and as blood began to run down her leg I thought she must be a virgin. In fact I am almost certain that the "priest" was wearing some sort of spiked ring around his penis which lacerated the woman as he entered her. She left the house shortly afterwards, and I was assured that one of the congregation was a doctor and would attend to her, but the dangers of blood poisoning, to say the least, were enormous.'

The evening ended with drunken dancing, drug taking, and general sexual activity, the partners circulating freely. Kordeiv, nauseated and frightened by what he had seen, left early and never returned.

He was fortunate; few Satanists would risk a member leaving their clutches and telling the police of what he had witnessed, and apart from physical violence they often use blackmail to prevent such an event. During the orgy a series of pictures are taken and the newly initiated member is solemnly warned that they will be made public should he not do as he is told. In any case Satanist cults often blackmail the new initiate to raise money for their organisation. In all, Satanist groups appear to be extremely unpleasant at best. At worst they are highly dangerous and, as author Denis Wheatley has often pointed out, are never to be lightly dallied with by anyone who values his freedom.

The Continental Satanists, such as the ones described above, are now widely imitated in America. The parody of the Mass is not hard for anyone to perform, black candles, robes, and the rest of the paraphenalia are obtainable by most people who desire to set up in practice on their own and – perhaps most important of all – the 'permissive society' in its boredom with normal sex readily yields up would-be participants in the obscene ceremonies.

It is perhaps typical that only in England, in stolid, down to earth Manchester, self-confessed Satanists attempt to give their beliefs a gloss of respectability. Here, in suburban homes, an extraordinary group who call themselves the 'Order of Satanic Templars' meet on several nights a week to worship Satan, who to them is still a glorious Prince of Heaven.

The Order of Satanic Templars is led by a bespectacled, dark suited man who refers to himself as 'Ramon'. A plasterer by trade, 'Ramon' has dabbled in most religions during the last twenty or so years, and, dissatisfied with them all, finally decided to organise his own particular branch of Satanism. He refers to his group as a 'coven' and claims that affiliated 'covens' exist throughout East Lancashire and Cheshire. Ramon's principal labour of love at the moment is his three volume 'Bible' which he refers to as the 'Black Book of Satan'. It contains a history of occultism, a list of rules for members attempting services at the Order's 'temple', several Satanic hymns – two or three of which are adapted versions of Christians hymns – and an account of his own philosophy.

'We believe,' says Ramon, 'that Satan, although thrown out of heaven, was reinstated as the son of God and is directly in contact with him. We are a bit evil now and again – if any of our coven members offends he is either reprimanded, given corporal punishment, or is expelled from his coven and cursed. But we only do this sort of thing for our members' own good. We really believe in love, the sanctity of woman as the child bearer and procreator of life, and in worshipping Satan our master. We don't go in for Black Masses or public intercourse or anything like that.'

Ramon has worked out a highly complex hierarchy with which to rule his little empire. He, as head of the 'Order' is aided by a council composed of chosen members of the other covens, and together they decide on policy and business matters. They wear black gowns – Ramon insisted on his wife re-designing the ones worn by male members as they were, he says, 'too effeminate' – and even children are allowed to attend meetings. 'We have the greatest reverence for children, and we would never go about naked in front of them, or do anything to harm them.'

To give him his due, Ramon's organisation seems very far removed from the wild and dangerous Satanists of other countries. Nonetheless, the ordinary people of Manchester apparently give him a wide berth.

7
Witchcraft in America

THE Salem witch trials of the late 17th century left a lasting mark on the North American continent, providing the background to innumerable books, plays, films, and political satires. The severe punishments meted out to the principals seem not only to have horrified onlookers of the day, but to have suppressed 'cult' witchcraft for over 250 years.

But the turmoil of the fifties produced a new attitude to witchcraft. As in other Western countries, people were turning again to religion but not, apparently, finding what they sought in its orthodox forms. Some young Americans looked to the East, to Buddhism, Mohammedanism, and the mystery religions of Tibet; others turned their attentions to a dark-haired, hawk-nosed, amply bosomed lady in her middle forties. Her name was Sybil Leek, she came from Hampshire, England, and the only thing which distinguished her at first sight from other, similar, ladies was an energetic jackdaw which perched on her shoulder and which rejoiced in the name 'Hotfoot Jackson'.

Mrs Leek settled in the United States in 1967 after a certain amount of trouble with her neighbours in the small town of Ringwood, in the New Forest. For Mrs Leek was a witch, and made no bones about it, and her antique shop in the town drew a good deal of attention from journalists and TV companies when the fact became known. According to legend the New Forest has always harboured witches. William Rufus, the Norman king held by some to have been a witch, was killed in a mysterious accident in the area and it was here, say the locals, that a band of witches met to turn back the invasion fleet of Napoleon by magic.

Following her British publicity, Mrs Leek received offers to appear on American television, and it is in America that she has made her home ever since. America, once so harsh with the Salem witches, has been good to Mrs Leek. Besides her now frequent radio and television interviews she has had her own show on both media, writes columns for the *Ladies Home Journal*, designs dresses for a chain of stores, lectures on occult matters – she became a strong rival to the Maharishi Mahesh Yogi during his brief period of fame by cornering the American market in transcendental meditation – and at one time planned to found a recording company. Amidst this flurry of commercial activity the witchcraft which started her off on the road to fame might well have been forgotten. But Mrs Leek stated otherwise after a burglar broke into her home in St Louis, Missouri, and stole three magic rings and a quantity of cash.

'If,' she announced sternly, 'the items are not returned within twenty-five days, the thief will live to rue the day. All hellishness will break loose. He does not realise what he has let himself in for by robbing me.'

The missing valuables were, apparently, returned well within the stated time ...

Mrs Leek, the enormous success of the film *Rosemary's Baby*, and the publicity given to witchcraft in general during the late sixties, served to dispel much of the fear of occult matters which had gathered throughout the United States since the Salem tragedies. Witchcraft, in various forms, has in fact almost become an 'in thing' nowadays, particularly among the young. New York's Greenwich Village area – always a hidden source of occult doings – broke out in a rash of fortune tellers, black magicians, astrologers, spirit mediums, ghost hunters, and witches of the 'Gardnerian' type as soon as the more permissive attitude to such subjects became apparent, while at the same time in other areas of the city, New York's hotch-potch of nations delved into their memories and produced the beliefs of their own, old, countries.

Though Greenwich Village is the 'trendy' centre of the new occult movement, with such newspapers as the famous *Village Voice* and the hippie-oriented *East Village Other* joining the 'underground' press in devoting advertising and editorial space to occultism in all its forms, witchcraft has become widely spread throughout the whole of greater New York. New York University has run lecture courses on the subject, as have various other educational establishments in New England – all of them well attended.

The sale of witchcraft items – books, ingredients for spells such as graveyard dirt, mandragora, and various herbs and spices, and of charms and amulets – has become literally a multi-million dollar business, not only in such areas as the Lower East Side and Harlem but in Park Lane itself. Many Wall Street businessmen are reported to carry specially 'hexed' charms about them nowadays and, as mentioned earlier, an increasing number of them habitually visit astrologers.

And it is businessmen, as well as fashionable artists, painters, and writers, who form the groups that secretly meet in richly decorated Westchester weekend homes and 'retreats' on Long Island – 'Great Gatsby' country – to perform rites which are based loosely on those described in the accounts of medieval witchcraft.

I say 'based loosely' because, like the Gardnerian rituals, they are invented to suit the particular group of people practising them. All kinds of activities are catered for – voyeurism, frotteurism, sado-masochism, and dozens of other sexual 'angles' can be worked into an occult 'ritual'. In one part of the area, the Mother Goddess may be worshipped to such an extent that the male members of the coven feel that they must prostrate themselves to her – in other words, the women beat the men; the reverse, of course, can be justified as easily. Another 'coven' may feel that sex in itself is the supreme act of worship, and practise either mass copulation or voyeurism, with the 'Priest' and 'Priestess' having sexual intercourse in the centre of the room while other members of the coven stand around and watch. Unlike their British counterparts, the American modern witches tend to be from a wealthy strata of society, and their robes, equipment, and meeting places reflect this wealth, so that American coven meetings are, to say the least, a spectacle. These Eastern covens, despite their strong sexual overtones, are by and large harmless enough affairs. Their members seek their own gratification without harming outsiders, and it is hard to obtain information on them, not because they are ashamed of what they do, but because they jealously guard their privacy and scarcely ever proselytise at all.

It is on the west coast of America, in California, that the occult has bloomed with a deadly flower. The hippie cult, with its fascination for drug-induced mystical experience is not far removed from those early European witches who 'flew' through the air after taking amanita muscaria, an hallucinogenic fungus. Bigger and better 'trips' on 'acid' – LSD – are the main purposes of life in these hippie communities, and once 'high' on acid many hippie minds start to crack.

Literally hundreds of groups with a 'mystical' basis have been formed in San Francisco, Los Angeles, and the small towns in between, during the past few years, and because of their basis in drug taking all are potentially dangerous. Even the apparently harmless Zen-based cults, with their strict but often unscientific methods of fasting, are likely to damage their own health if no one else's, and at the other end of the scale the terror gangs such as the Hell's Angels are a real and deadly menace to society.

Some of these new mystical religions are laughable at first sight; one woman, who claims that she is the reincarnation of an Egyptian Queen, calls herself Leda and entertains her followers by allowing a black swan to mount her naked body. According to magazine reports her house in Beverly Hills is sumptuous, and it is here that she 'rules' an assorted collection of heroin addicts, homosexuals, and psychopaths with ludicrous egocentricity. But even Leda has a dangerous side: it is her ambition to conduct a human sacrifice in the grounds of her house. She has a young man marked down as a suitable subject for immolation, and on several occasions has had him tied to a make-shift altar, with a razor sharp knife near at hand, only to decide against the murder at the last minute. It is possible that Princess Leda never intended to kill the young man, and that the whole thing is for theatrical effect. But the new, drug-crazed 'mystics' of California have killed, brutally and senselessly.

On the night of August 8, 1969, Charles Manson, an ex-convict turned self-styled 'prophet' who was referred to by his little bunch of followers as 'God', 'Jesus', and 'Satan', allegedly ordered Susan Atkins, Charles Watson, Patricia Krenwinkel, and Linda Kasabian to go to the home of the film director Roman Polanski on the outskirts of Los Angeles. According to Susan Atkins, reported in the *Los Angeles Times*, their orders were specific; to kill the occupants and steal any money or valuables on the premises. Manson reportedly had said that the expedition would be part of his campaign against 'straight' people.

Polanski himself – the director, ironically enough, of the film *Rosemary's Baby* – was away in Europe at the time, but his beautiful actress wife Sharon Tate was lying in bed, eight months pregnant, talking to her friend Jay Sebring, a fashionable hair stylist.

The four Manson followers were said to have scaled an iron fence surrounding the Polanski house and to have carefully cut all the telephone lines. Just inside the grounds they allegedly met eighteen-year-old Stephen Parent, a friend of the Polanski caretaker. When Parent tried to reach his car it was said that Watson drew a .22 pistol and shot him. Watson, according to Susan Atkins, was the only member of the party with a firearm; the girls carried knives and bayonets.

After ascertaining that Parent was dead, it was alleged that Watson entered the house through an open window and unlocked the front door. Linda Kasabian has since testified that she stayed outside while the two other girls went in. Inside, Voiteck Frykowski, a friend of the Polanski's, was asleep on a couch, but awoke and asked 'Who are you?'

'I am the devil,' was the alleged answer. 'I'm here to kill,' and Watson reportedly overpowered Frykowski and tied him securely.

Sharon Tate and Jay Sebring were then found in the bedroom, and they and coffee heiress Abigail Folger, who was in another bedroom, were dragged into the living room where they were tied together. Watson is reported to have then told the victims that they were going to die and when Sebring began to scream, to have shot him. Later on he was also stabbed and sexually mutilated. Frykowski, who had managed to loosen his bonds, made a dash for the front door but it is said Watson hit him over the head with his pistol, and then shot and stabbed him. Abigail Folger was then allegedly stabbed by Patricia Krenwinkel. When Susan Atkins refused to kill Sharon Tate, Watson is reported to have ripped into the actress with his knife. Her breasts were mutilated, and her body, together with that of Jay Sebring, was tied to a beam and left hanging there.

Outside, the intruders found that Abigail Folger had staggered onto the lawn and it was there that she was finally stabbed to death.

A policeman who saw the scene next morning expressed a little of the horror that shook the world later. A hardened officer who had served most of his life in a hard area, he was white when he came out of the house to tell reporters: 'I am sick, just sick to my stomach. I have seen some things but this . . . this is a bloodbath.'

More murders followed before the Manson gang were arrested. 'The Family' or 'Satan's Slaves' as they called themselves, had killed a total of twenty-five people, according to the Los Angeles police.

Manson and his followers are, at the time of writing, standing accused of these crimes. But what could have made anyone do it? Drugs obviously came into it, but Manson really appears to have believed that he was the Devil incarnate. His followers accepted him as such and, on his orders, are alleged to have performed not only murders but every kind of perverse and bestial sexual act for his gratification. It is not too fanciful to compare him with the 'Man in Black' of medieval witchcraft – the man who gave the orders posing as the Devil, though never carrying out the acts himself. In the Middle Ages, witches reported to the 'Devil' the evil that they had done since the last Sabbat; so Manson's followers did to him. The witches of old were 'rewarded' by having sex with the 'Devil'; Manson rewarded his followers in a similar fashion.

But a witch like Isobel Gowdie, burned in Scotland in the 17th century, appears pallid and insignificant in comparison with say Linda Kasabian; and perhaps only Gilles de Rais could match up to Manson himself for sheer, twisted evil.

East coast American witchcraft, cosy, slightly 'naughty' British witchcraft, bear no resemblance to the Manson devil cult. Perhaps it is only in the lurid, baking oven that is the Californian desert where the 'Family' made their home that such horror could take root in the mind of a man, making him feel that evil was good, that death was life, and that he himself was the Prince of Darkness.

8

Witchcraft Healing

... but it happened that my father became ill since May, and he was taken to Msume Hospital, there he stayed for two weeks or more. As the doctor examined him he found that the sickness was really terrible, so he took him to Mneni which is our biggest hospital down to our place. And so I had to go and see him there, and tried to talk to him, but he couldn't answer a word. He was ever lying in his bed ... after three weeks time I received a phone call from the sister nurse saying that my father was really finished and mama wants to take him away before he dies. ... Mama decided not to take him home but to take him to his cousin which is at Ruswinge. ... I never thought we would arrive Dadaya before he died on the way. Well I had asked the sister and she said he had the meningitis which is something about the brain, so I found a witch-doctor near Wedya on the way to the cousin, and he treated him. Dad started to get better and was OK. Nowadays he is much better than ever before, I think, so we hope him to be well for good now...

The above is the text of a letter sent to Judith Todd, daughter of former Rhodesian Prime Minister Garfield Todd, by a young African girl from her hometown.

The girl was sixteen, fairly well educated, and used to a Western style of life. But when her father became grievou. her instinct told her what to do – the witchdoctor was the answer. Almost certainly, psychosomatic healing played a part in the old man's recovery, but the recovery was remarkable nonetheless.

The healing witchdoctor is not indigenous to Africa alone. In Italy, almost all 'witches' are healing witches – when they are not laying curses or making love charms. In rural England, village wise men and women, the descendants of many of the lonely old women burned for their acts of mercy in former times, still ply the old trades. Many of their cures are based on herbal medicine. It was the 'witches' of England who, many years before the discovery of penicillin, recommended that a rotted piece of leather or a mouldy chunk of cheese be placed over a festering sore to cure it. They seem to have known instinctively that the mould culture on such substances held remarkable healing powers. Again, witches prescribed potions containing fox-gloves for heart disorders; in recent years digitalis, contained in the fox-glove flower, has been used extensively by doctors in heart drugs.

Apart from the purely natural healing performed by 'witches' there are also remarkable instances of healing by suggestion, hypnosis, 'magic' – call it what you will. The modern spiritualist faith healers, despite their protests to the contrary, are not much removed from their counterparts in witchcraft; the faith healers claim that their cures come from God, usually acting through the medium of a friendly spirit guide, while the witches claim that the power comes from 'outside', conjured up by incantations and spells and channelled into the afflicted person.

Forty years or so ago, England still had more than its fair share of 'wart curers'. These people usually filled the double roll of veterinary surgeon and doctor, delivering babies, healing sick cattle, charming away aches and pains, but their speciality lay in getting rid of warts. Why warts should loom so large, no one seems to know; recently, however, medical science has claimed that certain physical afflictions can be affected favourably by hypnosis – often unconscious self-hypnosis.

Until a couple of years ago, Looe, in Cornwall, had a wart curer of almost legendary powers; people visited him from all over the Cornish peninsula. His name was Dan Wickett. One of his patients runs a pottery shop today in Looe's main street, and although he still claims that Dan's reputation was based on a 'lot of mumbo-jumbo' he does admit to having had a 'wart the size of a sixpence' eradicated by the old man.

I was sitting on the quay one morning with some of the lads, old Dan among them. Since I was a child, I'd had a big wart on my left knee, and when the conversation came round to Dan's power I mentioned it to him. 'Where abouts is it,' said he. 'Here,' said I, and pointed to the spot. He pressed his thumb down on my trouser leg, just on the place, but through my trouser leg, mind. A couple of days later I was sitting in the bath, and the thing had gone. Damned if I knew how he did it. I'd forgotten about the incident. I asked him later if he'd teach me how to do the same, but he told me he'd already promised the power to somebody else when he passed on.

So according to Dan the hereditary aspect of the craft was still present. In Italy, the hereditary aspect is even more firmly entrenched. There, witches usually run in families, and there is rarely any shame or secrecy attached to the profession of the craft. In Northern Italy, where Leland found much of his material for *Aradia* eighty years ago, industry has driven out many of the old beliefs, but in the South, in Sicily and Calabria, nearly every hamlet has its 'strega' or witch. Like the old village wise women of Britain, the streghe fulfil many roles in the community, often acting even as marriage guidance councillors. They are sometimes paid in cash, at other times in kind – ranging from a few eggs to a cow.

Although 'witch-families' abound, not everyone is 'born' a witch. Many are taught by their mothers before they reach their twentieth birthday – the day of maturity for Italian sorceresses. With few exceptions, the streghe are women, reflecting the highly matriarchal Italian life style. There are various omens at the birth of a 'natural' witch. A child born in a caul has minor powers, slightly less than those possessed by a premature seven-month child. If it is born on the seventh day of the seventh month of its mother's pregnancy, its powers are even stronger, and perhaps strongest of all are the in-built gifts of a seventh daughter. As in other parts of the world a 'Christmas baby', particularly if born at midnight on Christmas

Eve, is especially gifted, and curiously enough, despite
the fact that Shakespeare claims that 'no witch hath
power to charm' on Christmas Day, such children are
noted for their cursing abilities. Although Italian
witches will often talk, almost boast, of their methods,
few will tell of cursing or killing methods on any other
than Christmas Day.

Writing on Italian witchcraft, the American author,
C. H. Wallace, remarked on the curious names possessed by the streghe; Carminella La Lupa (Carminella
the She-Wolf), Sabella La Ricciotta (Sabella the Curly
Haired One), Zelinda La Buona (Zelinda the Good),
Concetta La Praticona (Concetta the Experienced)
and, perhaps significantly, Zaira La Boira (Zaira the
Executioner). Often the witches take their names from
their place of birth; the Italian Dr Carlo Levi, exiled
under Mussolini to a tiny village in the South, described in his book *Christ Stopped at Eboli* his strange
friendship with a witch who served as his housekeeper
– another Italian tradition of long standing: only
witches can keep house for bachelors. Dr Levi's com-
panion was named Giulia di Sant' Angelo, because she
was born in Sant' Angelo, although her 'practice' was
in Gagliano.

A characteristic of Italian streghe is that they
scarcely, if ever, specialise in black or white magic –
magic is magic, to be used for whatever purpose is
necessary at the moment. Some make love philtres,
some cure cattle, some charm spirits, some either turn
on or turn away the evil eye, and some perform
straightforward cursing jobs, often with fatal results.

These results, however, are not often achieved by straight witchcraft for, in the tradition of the Medicis, the Italian streghe have always been noted for their skill in brewing deadly and rarely detectable poisons.

Like witches in other parts of the world, the Italian variety often go in for fortune telling. One of the most successful is, oddly enough, a man – known in Italy as Il Mago di Napoli, the Magician of Naples. An aristocrat and professional diplomat, Il Mago is in constant demand by students of the Naples University wishing to know the results of examinations – which shows that witchcraft still flourishes in the upper as well as lower echelons of Italian society.

North of the border, in France, witchcraft has recently moved from the purely peasant level of its past to a rather 'in' position with the young jet set of the Riviera and Paris. Curiously it is not the sexual, ritual aspect of the subject which seems to fascinate the majority of most young French people, but the old herbal magic one. Pigalle is a centre, naturally, for love charms and philtres, most of which are made locally by otherwise quite respectable chemists. The same chemists often also stock various brands of herbal tea, each brand having a different property – one is good for rheumatism, another good for arthritis, while others have slightly more mystical connotations and are useful for attracting lovers, animals, money, and almost everything else.

A popular cure, smacking of vampire lore as well as traditional French cuisine, is for the common cold. Visit a 'wise woman' in Provence, for instance, and ask her to cure your cold, and she will prepare a mess of crushed garlic and, pronouncing suitable incantations, put it into a bag and hang it around your neck. Whether the garlic or the magical spell is mainly responsible few Frenchmen seem able to say, but most of them report that it works!

Germany, unlike France and Italy, with their still-largely rural outlook on life, is rather stern and humourless when it comes to witchcraft of any kind, let alone that practised by village witchdoctors. The rapid rebuilding and re-industrialisation programme of post-war West Germany has left most German people with a sternly practical outlook on life. When cult witchcraft is practised, mainly in Berlin and Hamburg, it is highly sexual in content, with strong sado-masochistic overtones – black leather, whips, and chains being the order of the day.

But there are pockets of village-style sorcery even in Germany, though sadly, the general opinion of such local witches is not dissimilar to that which prevailed in Britain, say, during the great witch persecutions. An English television director who made a short film of the British witch Alex Sanders for showing on West German television was delighted at the popularity of his work there. But the German producer told him, after the film was screened: 'It is a pity. I think the Church in England was not ruthless enough in rooting out witches in your country.'

This was said entirely without humour. For Germans have re-initiated their own 'rooting out' activities against witches only recently. In the early sixties twenty-six-year-old Johann Vogel was sentenced to prison in Bamberg, North Bavaria, for attempting to burn to death a sixty-four-year-old woman in the village of Mailach in Hessen. The woman, Elizabeth Hahn, lived in a little house alone and, as it appeared at the trial, ostracised by most of the villagers. Vogel had been ill for some time, and, deciding that Elizabeth Hahn had bewitched him, set fire to her house. Fortunately she escaped the flames but her house and all her possessions were totally destroyed. Sentencing Vogel, the presiding judge ruled that Elizabeth Hahn was a 'harmless and lonely old person who only needed human kindness', a verdict which could have equally applied to most of the 9,000,000 so-called 'witches' slaughtered in Europe during the times of persecution.

It is just possible, in the absence of medical evidence to the contrary, that Elizabeth Hahn did put a 'curse' on Vogel – or rather that her very existence in the village and Vogel's belief that she was a witch did so. For fear is an essential ingredient of a curse, just as faith is vital for psychosomatic healing. One may dismiss the notion that fear of magic could paralyse a modern, educated human being, but the fact is that, with a little elementary psychology, almost anyone can cast a spell on almost anyone else. A London psychiatrist whose interest runs to magic and witchcraft explained: 'If I told even an average layman that I was a witch and had put a fatal curse on him, he would probably just laugh. But if I told him, with a suitable expression of horror, that I had accidentally poured a deadly poison into his gin and that he would die within five minutes, it is highly likely that he would suffer severe stomach cramps, headache, and nausea. Knowing that I am a doctor, he would probably just take my word for it: and that's the way that magic – curative or malicious – works.'

The deeper ingrained the belief, the more readily does the effect take hold. In 1967 Colonel Ojukwu, the Biafran leader, ordered a £350,000 Hawker Siddeley jet from a firm in Luton, Bedfordshire. At Lagos, where the plane made a fuelling stop, a man ran out from the perimeter of the airfield and scattered white powder around the aircraft, muttering incantations. Ojukwu, a man with the highest military training, refused delivery on the grounds that the plane was bewitched.

Obviously, the emergent nations of Africa are still more widely in thrall to witchcraft than most European countries, and on several occasions, unscrupulous landlords have used the fear of magic to control immigrant tenants. There have been times when immigrants have used magic to scare each other. In 1967, Mr K. W. Robbins, clerk of the London Borough of Harringay, was approached by a poor West Indian who said that an African family sharing his house in Hornsey had pinned a spell to his door. Mr Robbins approached Mrs Helen Carlisle, head of the Council Advice Bureau, and she 'dashed off a note on Council headed notepaper asking the family to come and see her. I told the West Indian that this was better magic than anything his neighbours had,' she said. 'He wasn't troubled again.'

9
King of the Witches

As we have seen, almost every country in the Western
world has its witches today, and their numbers are
steadily growing. Some, like the Magician of Naples,
Sybil Leek in America, and the late Gerald Gardner,
have become personalities in their own right, sym-
bolising to many laymen all the other, lesser, members
of the curious craft. But if these three have achieved
a measure of international success, they are being
rapidly overtaken by the most flamboyant witch of
them all, an Englishman who claims he is King of the
Witches, and swears that one day he will make 'Aleister
Crowley look like a boy scout'.

At first sight, the gaunt features with their convex,
impenetrably dark glasses are sinister in the extreme.
Above the tall narrow forehead, brown hair is brushed
forward in a Nero-like fashion, while the rest of the
figure, apart from the hands, is swathed in a cloak of
royal blue velvet, relieved only by a flash of gold braid
on the shoulders and a golden lunula or upturned
crescent moon over the left breast. The hands are
long-fingered and sensitive and the rings on them look

far too heavy. At second glance, with the blank black spectacles removed, Alex Sanders looks anything but sinister. The rather sad brown eyes and finely modelled cheek bones give him a totally fragile, vulnerable appearance, an impression which is increased when he speaks in his soft Lancashire voice. 'I am King of the Witches,' he says in a flat, matter of fact tone, 'because I was elected by members of over one hundred covens in Britain, and I am recognised by most other covens as an authority on witchcraft.'

He calculates that there are about four thousand witches in Britain, a number which is increasing daily, and believes that there are six families of 'hereditary' witches, including his own.

The last man to call himself King of the Witches, according to Alex, was Owain Glyn Dwr, the medieval Welsh chieftain. Alex's maternal grandmother, a Mrs Bibby, made researches and discovered that she was a direct descendant of Glyn Dwr; it was by her that Alex was initiated into the first degree of witchcraft.

'One evening in 1933, when I was seven, I was sent round to my grandmother's house for tea,' he recalls. 'For some reason I didn't knock on the door as I went in, and was confronted by my grandmother, naked, with her grey hair hanging down below her waist, standing in a circle drawn on the kitchen floor. A number of curious objects surrounded her. There were swords, a black-handled knife, a sickle-shaped knife, and various brass bowls lying around on the floor; other odd objects lay on the large Welsh dresser which stood against one wall.'

For once, Alex's grandmother did not seem pleased
to see him. Recovering her composure, she ordered him
to step into the circle and remove his clothes. Shaking
with fright, he did so. His grandmother ordered him
to bend over with his head between his naked thighs.
Then, taking up the sickle-knife, she nicked his
scrotum slightly. 'You are one of us now,' she said,
and Alex suddenly realised his grandmother was a
witch.

Gradually, his fear vanished and he began to visit
her house regularly. She taught him to develop his
powers of clairvoyance, to cast simple spells, to study,
to learn. But she also swore him to secrecy; no one, not
even his mother – Mrs Bibby's daughter – must know
of the skills he was being taught.

'On my tenth birthday,' recalls Alex, 'my grandmother fulfilled a long standing promise to take me to
London. After showing me the sights she introduced
me to a man named "Mr Alexander" and left me with
him at a small boarding house, where he told me he
was a master magician and performed a ritual which
he called "The Rites of Horus". It was not until I was
sixteen that I realised that "Mr Alexander" was, in
fact, Aleister Crowley.'

Today, Alex bears a memento of this singular occasion on the second finger of his left hand. It is a finely
engraved silver seal ring which Crowley gave to Mrs
Bibby in trust for Alex, and which formerly belonged
to the 19th-century French magician Eliphas Lévi.

Mrs Bibby died in 1942 and, true to the instructions
she had given him, Alex burned her copy of the 'Book

of Shadows' a document which, he says, is copied out by every witch in his or her own hand, and destroyed on the death of its owner. Fortunately, he was able to preserve some of her 'working tools' – her athame, or black handled knife, her sword, and various other items of equipment. Before she died, Alex's grandmother had initiated him up to the 'third degree' – which involved his having token sexual intercourse with her. After the Second World War, finding himself isolated by the occult knowledge she had imparted to him, he decided to use these powers to procure money and sex by witchcraft. 'I made a dreadful mistake in using black magic in an attempt to bring myself wealth and sexual success,' he says. 'It worked all right – I was walking through Manchester and I was accosted by a middle-aged couple who told me that I was an exact double of their only son, who had died some years previously. They took me into their home, fed and clothed me, and treated me as one of the family. They were extremely wealthy and, in 1952, when I asked them for a house of my own, with an allowance to run it on, they were quite happy to grant my wishes. I held parties, bought expensive clothes, I was sexually promiscuous; but it was only after a time that I realised I had a fearful debt to pay.'

The debt was harrowing and personal. Several members of the Sanders family died of cancer, and finally one of Alex's mistresses, a girl of whom he was particularly fond, committed suicide. Alex held himself to blame. 'I felt ashamed of betraying my grandmother's teaching,' he recalls. 'It took me a long time to purge my guilt and purify myself, through the medium of magical ceremonies.'

Once convinced that his past life lay behind him, and that his true vocation lay in teaching others the creed of his grandmother, Alex set to work to initiate would-be witches in his home town of Manchester. He was on his own at this time, two previous marriages having come to an end. During the course of his teaching he met and married a girl named Maxine Morris, who is now his High Priestess, and by whom he has a baby, Maya.

In 1967 they left Manchester and settled in London, and it is there, in a flat in Notting Hill Gate, that they have lived and worked ever since. Every Tuesday and Thursday Alex holds meetings to instruct new witches; while Saturday evenings are devoted to coven meetings and initiations. He claims that among the followers of his doctrine are orthodox ministers, doctors, theological students, teachers, and journalists. Since he came to London he has initiated thirty-eight witches – all women, for it is part of the witch's creed that only a male witch can initiate a female candidate; the would-be male witch is initiated by Maxine, the High Priestess. His teachings, he claims, are not incompatible with Christianity, provided that students remember that 'all monotheist religions are worshipping the one God'. Like most witches he believes in reincarnation, and holds ceremonies to honour the four seasons, the equinoxes and solstices, as well as carrying out small personal acts of worship at sunrise and sunset. Again, like other witches, his followers conduct their meetings in the nude, although Alex himself wears a robe to set himself apart as High Priest; he says that this is in accordance with witchcraft law. Despite his early black magic extravagances, he nowadays lives the life of an ordinary married man. The only sexual aspects of his rituals occur during the 'Great Rite' ceremony of third degree initiation, when the initiate undergoes token intercourse, and at 'witch weddings'.

The celebration of 'witch weddings' involves the two partners lying together in the middle of the circle, while the other members surround them facing outwards. After incantations have been performed by the High Priest the couple are left alone to consummate their union. This done, they call the rest of the coven into the room for an informal cakes and wine ceremony.

Perhaps far more dramatic than any of the private ceremonies which Alex Sanders performs is the fact that, in little more than a year, he has become a public figure of almost pop star status. One of the more sensational Sunday newspapers denounced him in 1969; but this only served to stimulate the other media into giving him a publicity boost that would have cost thousands of pounds had he employed an advertising agency. A book on his life entitled *King of the Witches*, published in 1959, became a steady seller. A film entitled *Legend of the Witches* featured Alex's activities, including reconstructions of a Black Mass and the creation of a doll for the purposes of witchcraft — practices which he has now abandoned. Despite the fact that many people in the cinema world believed that it would never be released, the film drew capacity audiences in London's West End. A pop group who featured magical rituals in their act and who were taken under Alex's wing – 'they were far too accurate in their conjurations,' he explained, 'and I felt I ought to protect them' – sold hundreds of records on the strength of Alex's patronage. A long-playing record of his rituals was released by the American company A & M Records. Jimmy Saville, a disc jockey famous both in Britain and on the Continent, featured him on a controversial radio interview, and a TV appearance on the popular 'Simon Dee Show' during which Alex demonstrated a magical 'killing' technique drew huge correspondence. Perhaps even more remarkable was the result of an interview that Alex had with Joan Bakewell on BBC's 'Late Night Line Up'. Mrs Bakewell is widely regarded among Britain's viewers as a beautiful blue-stocking, reflecting the programme's involvement with the arts and with all manner of intellectual activity. A member of the programme's team said later that Joan Bakewell and other members of the production unit had found Alex, 'most professional as a performer and most impressive as a person. The whole of the programme's crew were impressed – even more so when the switchboard was jammed in a matter of minutes after Alex's appearance by people asking for his help. We had expected a few protest telephone calls, but the reaction we got was just the opposite. Alex Sanders is a very extraordinary man.'

As a result of his British appearances, Alex has appeared on several Continental television pro-

grammes. In Germany, after a film of him being interviewed in Sir Francis Dashwood's 'Hell Fire Caves',
reaction was enthusiastic. Letters flooded in from
modern 'covens' asking for the address of 'The Master'.
The impression which Alex Sanders makes on people
who meet him or see him on television seems to be a
magnetic one, whether or not they believe in his
alleged magical powers. Certainly no occultist has
created such a stir since Aleister Crowley died nearly
a quarter of a century ago.

Alex himself, hiding behind his sinister black glasses
and his alternating fits of shrewd humour, seriousness,
cynicism, and undoubted showmanship, remains an
enigma.

From the spirit-raising witch of Endor to a 'pop' witch
such as Alex Sanders is a long step: chronologically
at least. But the witches of classical and biblical times
and their modern counterparts who cavort nude in
cosy sitting-rooms do have much in common. The
belief in an outside agency, a power which can be
tapped and used for good or evil, a power which can
elevate them in the minds of their fellow beings to the
position almost of demi-gods, is common to both. And
the use of psychological tricks to win 'clients' is as old
as the ages.

Despite all the publicity, the near hysteria of the
popular press, the questions on witchcraft asked in the
British House of Commons, it is my firm conviction
that no 'witch' can summon up enough magical power
to boil a kettle of water. On the other hand, irrespon-

sible elements in witchcraft can be extremely dangerous to the weak minded and superstitious.

Not all modern covens are essentially bad or particularly good. Like the magic which they so firmly believe in, most of them are neutral.

One High Priestess said: 'Witchcraft, despite its trappings, is just another way of life. The Horned God and Mother Goddess whom we worship symbolise the creative forces which made the universe, and which our ancestors worshipped long ago. Our religion has the same purpose as other religions. We worship as our fathers worshipped before us. I think that is fairly reasonable, don't you?'

Perhaps the whole question is best left there.

Further Reading

St Thomas Aquinas, *Opuscula*
Apuleius, *The Golden Ass*
    De Magia
Francis Bacon, *Sylva Sylvarum*, Longman, 1870
E. M. Butler, *Ritual Magic*, Cambridge, 1959
Richard Cavendish, *The Black Arts*, Routledge &
    Kegan Paul, 1967
John Evelyn, *Diary*, Dent, 1966
Sir J. G. Frazer, *The Golden Bough*, Macmillan, 1922
G. B. Gardner, *Witchcraft Today*, Arrow Books, 1966
Robert Graves, *The White Goddess*, Faber & Faber,
    1952
T. Hobbes, *Leviathan*
Christina Hole, *Witchcraft in England*, Collier-Mac-
    millan, 1967
Matthew Hopkins, *The Discovery of Witches*
Horace, *Satires*
Aldous Huxley, *The Devils of Loudon*, Chatto &
    Windus, 1961
J. Johns, *King of the Witches*, Peter Davies, 1969

H. C. Lea, *Materials Towards a History of Witchcraft*, 1939

    A History of the Inquisition of Spain, 1967

Lucan, *The Pharsalia*

L. Mair, *Witchcraft*, Weidenfeld & Nicolson, 1969

Eric Maple, *The Dark World of Witches*, Pan, 1965

    Domain of Devils, Robert Hale, 1966

Margaret Murray, *The Witch Cult in Western Europe*, Oxford, 1963

    God of the Witches

H. T. F. Rhodes, *The Satanic Mass*, Arrow Books, 1965

Stephen Runciman, *A History of the Crusades*, Cambridge, 1952–4

    The Medieval Manichee, Cambridge, 1947

Ronald Seth, *In the Name of the Devil*, Jarrolds, 1969

J. Sprenger and H. Kramer, *Malleus Maleficarum*, Hogarth, 1951

Montague Summers, *Witchcraft and Black Magic*, Rider, 1946

A. E. Waite, *The Book of Black Magic and of Pacts*, 1898

ABOUT THE AUTHOR

Frank Smyth was born and educated in Yorkshire, and now edits the 'Frontiers of Belief' section in *Man, Myth & Magic*. He is a freelance writer, having worked on *The Yorkshire Post* and the *Record Retailer*, of which he was editor. He has handled the publicity for various well-known pop-groups. He has written children's stories, and has contributed short stories to anthologies and articles to magazines. He lives in London.

ACKNOWLEDGMENTS

We are grateful to the following for permission to use copyright prints and photographs:

Jacqueline Mackay, 5; Mansell Collection, 4; National Film Archive, 10; Prof. E. Evans Pritchard, 6; Radio Times Hulton Picture Library, 1, 2, 9; William Sargant, 7; Syndication International, 8; John Webb, 3.

The quotation from the musical *Hair* is reproduced by permission of United Artists Music Ltd.